The Rewilding Yearbook

A 12-month journey to discover the wild within you

Illustrated by
Rachael Roux

MADDY WINTERBROOK
& ELEANOR CHEETHAM

VERBENA

CONTENTS

WELCOME TO YOUR REWILDING YEAR...

In ecological terms, 'rewilding' means restoring a natural habitat to its intrinsic state by reintroducing lost species, encouraging organic processes, and scaling back human intervention. Rewilded ecosystems are supported both to thrive autonomously, shaped and sustained by their own inherent life force, and to coexist in harmony with the wider world. This is how the concept relates to outer nature, but what if we apply it to our inner nature, the metaphorical landscape of the self?

This book is a guide to personal rewilding: an invitation to recover your natural state; your innate sense of who you truly are. Just as a forest or river becomes more vibrant when given the freedom to flourish on its own terms, so too can we humans become more alive when we allow ourselves to follow a wilder path. For centuries, advances in science and industry have helped us develop as a species, but defining growth solely in terms of productivity means that 'human nature' (once understood as a deep connection to the wild world) has become more about screens and spreadsheets than seasons and sunsets. The spark of aliveness in our hearts has dwindled to an ember, but it's still glowing there, ready to be rekindled.

Slowly but surely, we're beginning to question the long-established interpretations of what it means to be human: not an unyielding cog in a machine, but a soft-bodied, intuitive animal. The status quo (shaped by the Enlightenment and the Industrial Revolution) is being critically examined, and the idea of taking a different path – a wilder path – is now taking root. We're challenging the (Western) cultural narrative that places humans at the top of the hierarchy and defines 'nature' and 'the environment' as separate and other; a resource to be dominated and exploited.

In its place, a rewilded perspective is unfurling that positions humans as an equal part of the interconnected web of life and also embraces the land beyond our walls and windows as our home. Of course, this approach has informed the relationships of many Indigenous communities with the earth for millennia and is not a 'new' idea at all, but a welcome return to time-honoured ways of being that have always been there.

We find ourselves at a fork in the road, with the well-trodden 'way it's always been' luring us in one direction and this new, perhaps more winding, path beckoning us in another. Facing a global climate emergency, a mental health crisis, and a culture of workplace burnout, we can either keep going in the same way, hoping for a different result, or fully embrace the nature-inspired alternative that could lead to meaningful change. Deep ecologist Joanna Macy refers to this decisive moment as the Great Turning, calling for a collective 'greening of the self' to heal the human–nature divide. At The Wild Academy, we think of this identity shift as the cultivation of the *wild self*.

Unearthing this part of ourselves is not easy, and there are many reasons why it may feel buried, lost, or unsafe to reveal. Look up 'wild' in the dictionary and this resistance begins to make sense: 'uncontrolled, violent, or extreme' says one source; 'uncivilised or barbarous' says another. Most definitions refer to hostile wastelands, 'primitive' instincts, a sense of unfamiliarity that is feared or exoticised, or an irrepressible force that is volatile and possibly dangerous. Descriptions like this make us think of wild beasts, wild weather, wildfire, wild tempers: unbridled chaos, distress, damage, and rage.

And then there's wild women. When you apply such ideas to the female character, undoubtedly as a consequence of the historic persecution of witches, the resulting associations lead straight to a string of tired stereotypes: emotional, hysterical, rebellious, outspoken, immoral. Much like wild landscapes, 'untamed' women (and indeed all people labelled by society as 'unruly' in some way) have long been viewed as uncontrolled and therefore uncontrollable.

Through this lens, the choice to embrace rather than suppress our intrinsic wildness can be tinged with fear and shame, making it easy to see why many of us may struggle at first to feel safe and free enough to access this part of ourselves.

So, what if we choose to think of wildness in a different way? There are alternative meanings that spark thoughts of free-spirited adventure, breathtaking views, untouched beauty, innate knowing, and expansive possibilities. Wild horses, wild landscapes, wildflowers, wildest dreams. Through this lens, the call of the wild becomes an invitation to return to the earth and reclaim our roots: unburdened, uninhibited, *untamed*. Embracing our wild self means shedding the layers of social and cultural conditioning that tell us who to be and committing to discovering that for ourselves, with nature's wisdom as our lantern in the dark.

How, you ask? That's where this book comes in! Structured as a journey through the year, it's intended to guide you as you walk the wild path, offering insights and explorations to help you connect with the seasons and cycles both around and within you. Rewilding is about going beyond surface-level nature connection and seeking a deeper relationship with the earth and with the self. Designed to be immersive and experiential, we hope this book will be a trusted companion on your pilgrimage of wild becoming; your North Star to find your way home.

HOW TO USE THIS BOOK

The book is based on the framework of our Rewilding Wheel (more on this shortly) and is split into four seasons, beginning with winter. Each of these seasonal quarters opens with a short summary of its key themes and qualities, before being further divided into monthly chapters – of which there are three per season (so 12 in total). Our allocation of months to seasons may surprise you if you're not familiar with the Wheel of the Year, but you'll learn more about this as we go along!

Each monthly chapter explores its corresponding segment of the Rewilding Wheel, weaving information with practical tasks and prompts to help you connect to its meanings. You could move through each month in turn, in line with the real-time unfolding of the year, or you might choose to start at a point that feels intuitive to you, such as January or your birth month. Alternatively, you may wish to dive into a section that fits the metaphorical 'season' of your life. As with all things wild, there are no set rules or expectations, and you should feel free to explore in your own way.

Follow Your Wild Intuition

Each chapter contains a range of practical activities to help you engage with the themes we explore. Some are designed to support contemplation through journalling or other reflective practices, while others involve creative projects or venturing outdoors. It is important to us that these 'exercises' are viewed not as instructions, but as invitations: gentle suggestions that can be taken up or passed by as needed. You will likely feel more drawn to some than others, and that's okay – giving yourself permission to trust and follow your wild intuition is a vital part of the rewilding process.

Similarly, we recognise and respect that all minds and bodies are different, as are all our circumstances, budgets, experiences of the seasons, and levels of access to nature. With this diversity in mind, we understand that not all the activities will necessarily be possible for everyone to follow in the way we suggest. Just as the plants and animals of the wild world are continually adapting to changing conditions, we warmly encourage you to find ways of connecting with the book that suit your individual needs and circumstances. Whether it's by tailoring our guidance or creating entirely new explorations, please feel free to use our suggestions as a starting point for forging your own unique path.

THE REWILDING WHEEL

The Rewilding Wheel is a tool designed to bring together various layers of nature-inspired wisdom in alignment with the cycle of the year. Centred around the four seasons, it draws on a number of different systems and ideas, which we'll outline in this section. Its surface-level purpose is to imbue each season (and the months within them) with a deep sense of resonance: an instinctive, felt understanding of what it means to move through the year. Beneath this, it also has the potential to offer a profound form of identity exploration, acting as both a map of the 'landscape' and a compass to guide your journey. Through cultivating greater awareness of the seasons, the Rewilding Wheel supports conscious connection with the self, with its symbols becoming metaphors for aspects of our personalities, lives, and experiences.

It's important to note that the Wheel is based on a Northern Hemisphere perspective, but its layers could easily be switched around to suit the Southern Hemisphere, if required. Similarly, our interpretation of the seasons is rooted in the British Isles and, while this will also be applicable to much of Northern Europe and some of North America, it won't reflect all regions of the world due to geographical differences. In line with our untamed philosophy, the Rewilding Wheel is a living framework, feral and ever-evolving. We encourage you to develop your own version inspired by the land where you live and your personal relationship with the wild world.

Rewilding Wheel Structure

The Rewilding Wheel's structure is based around the Wheel of the Year, which we explain a little later in this section. For now, simply note the eight seasonal festivals marked around the edge of the circle.

Each seasonal quarter has a set of overarching associations: an element (Earth, Air, Fire, Water), a soulscape (symbolic terrain), and a general archetype (aspect of self), which are all displayed in the centre of the circle, plus a direction and time of day, which can be seen at the four compass points around the edge. These correspondences relate to the entire season, providing a sense of the phase as a whole.

The four seasons are then subdivided into their three months. Reading from the outer layers of the Wheel and working inwards, you'll see that each monthly segment has its own guiding word (for example, November's is 'root' and June's is 'flourish'), seasonal symbol, named lunar cycle, tree, animal guide, and specific archetype (a facet of the wider seasonal identity).

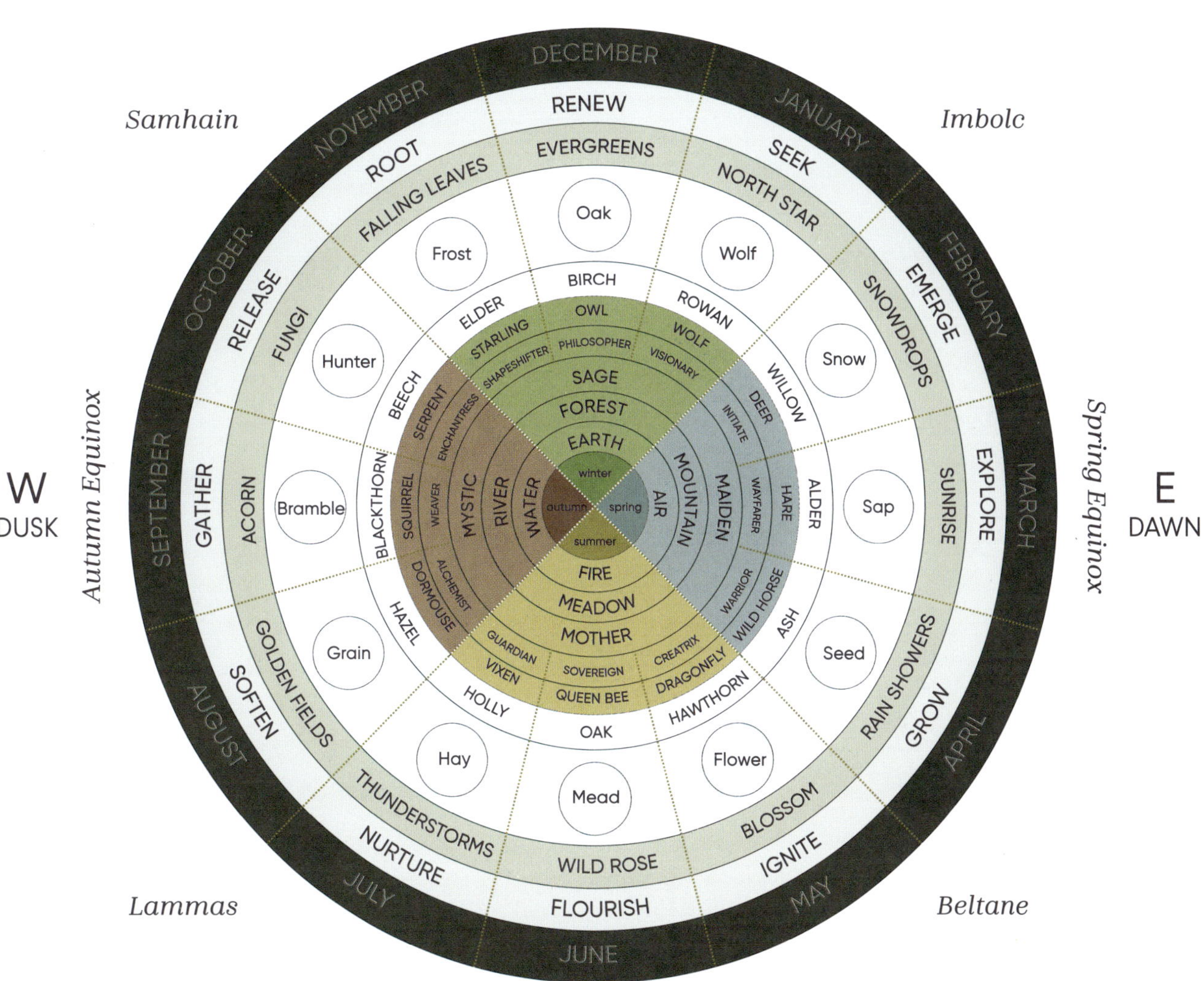
N
MIDNIGHT
Winter Solstice
Samhain
Imbolc
W
DUSK
Autumn Equinox
E
DAWN
Spring Equinox
Lammas
Beltane
Summer Solstice
MIDDAY
S
DECEMBER
JANUARY
FEBRUARY
MARCH
APRIL
MAY
JUNE
JULY
AUGUST
SEPTEMBER
OCTOBER
NOVEMBER
RENEW
SEEK
EMERGE
EXPLORE
GROW
IGNITE
FLOURISH
NURTURE
SOFTEN
GATHER
RELEASE
ROOT
EVERGREENS
NORTH STAR
SNOWDROPS
SUNRISE
RAIN SHOWERS
BLOSSOM
WILD ROSE
THUNDERSTORMS
GOLDEN FIELDS
ACORN
FUNGI
FALLING LEAVES
Oak
Wolf
Snow
Sap
Seed
Flower
Mead
Hay
Grain
Bramble
Hunter
Frost
BIRCH
ROWAN
WILLOW
ALDER
ASH
HAWTHORN
OAK
HOLLY
HAZEL
BLACKTHORN
BEECH
ELDER
OWL
WOLF
DEER
HARE
WILD HORSE
DRAGONFLY
QUEEN BEE
VIXEN
DORMOUSE
SQUIRREL
SERPENT
STARLING
PHILOSOPHER
VISIONARY
INITIATE
WAYFARER
WARRIOR
CREATRIX
SOVEREIGN
GUARDIAN
ALCHEMIST
WEAVER
ENCHANTRESS
SHAPESHIFTER
SAGE
MAIDEN
MOTHER
MYSTIC
FOREST
MOUNTAIN
MEADOW
RIVER
EARTH
AIR
FIRE
WATER
winter
spring
summer
autumn

Rewilding Wheel Components

The Wheel of the Year

The Wheel of the Year is an earth-centred calendar guided by the movement of the sun. It's often described as being Celtic in origin but is probably a modern conflation of ancient, nature-inspired traditions with neo-Pagan and Wiccan beliefs.

Differing from the Gregorian calendar, the Wheel of the Year begins and ends on the last day of October and divides the 12-month cycle into eight phases. These phases each span a period of six to eight weeks and are all marked at the start with a specific festival. These celebrations consist of the four fire festivals (or 'cross-quarter' days) of Samhain, Imbolc, Beltane, and Lammas and the four solar markers of the solstices (Winter and Summer) and equinoxes (Spring and Autumn).

The fire festivals are rooted in the prehistoric agricultural year of the Northern Hemisphere, and the British Isles in particular. They herald the transition into each season: Samhain brings winter on 31st October, Imbolc signals spring on 1st February, Beltane welcomes summer on 1st May, and Lammas honours the harvest that precedes autumn on 1st August. Although these dates may seem early, they offer gentle reminders that a different energy is emerging and the smallest signs of change are on the horizon.

Solstices and equinoxes are astronomical events that occur at a specific time each year, usually between the 20th and 23rd of their respective months: December and June for the Winter and Summer Solstices, then March and September for the Spring and Autumn Equinoxes. As important points of solar transition, these events have long been honoured across the world. They mark our arrival at the peak of each season, after which the energy of that phase begins to wane, until the next fire festival arrives and a new season starts to unfurl.

While the Rewilding Wheel follows this structure, the book doesn't include in-depth descriptions of the festivals themselves, as there are many other wonderful resources that cover their origins and customs – some of which we have listed in the closing pages. Instead, you will find the primary themes of these seasonal waymarkers woven throughout each chapter as we explore the symbolism of each month.

Elements, directions, times of day, and soulscapes

Each season is linked with an element (Earth, Air, Fire, Water), a direction (North, East, South, West), and a time of day (midnight, dawn, midday, dusk). These groupings originate from a historic set of correspondences codified in 19th-century Britain and differ from similar associations found in other cultures.

The seasons are also paired with a 'soulscape' – a landscape or habitat that we feel best reflects its unique essence. We've chosen these to emphasise the seasons' elemental qualities: the forest for winter (Earth), the mountains for spring (Air), the meadow for summer (Fire), and the river for autumn (Water).

As with the Wheel of the Year, all these aspects are integrated into the book's monthly chapters rather than receiving individual attention.

Archetypes and animal guides

The four primary archetypes at the centre of the Wheel have evolved from the traditional threefold grouping of the Maiden, Mother, and Crone personas, expanded and redefined as Sage, Maiden, Mother, and Mystic to correlate with the four seasons.

These have been further divided into 12 sub-archetypes, which pair with the months of the year. Inspired by archetypal depth psychology, these draw on all kinds of sources – from myths to our own experiences – and offer a more nuanced exploration of identity throughout the cycle.

Additionally, the sub-archetypes are each matched with an animal guide to further illuminate their qualities, and to create an opportunity to seek guidance from the more-than-human world.

Trees

Each month is paired symbolically with a particular tree. This concept is based on something known as the Celtic Tree Calendar, which was largely developed by the 20th-century English writer Robert Graves. In his book *The White Goddess*, he explored an early medieval script called Ogham (pronounced 'oh-am'), often described informally as the Celtic Tree Alphabet, as its rune-like symbols are believed by some to represent the names of trees. Graves' calendar was informed by his interpretations of Ogham characters, and we've used this idea as the foundation for our approach. The trees we have included are based on a combination of the original Celtic Tree Calendar, the work of author and artist Glennie Kindred, and our own relationships with the natural world.

Moons

The 12 circles within the Wheel represent the year's lunar cycles. The practice of naming full moons can be found across many Indigenous cultures worldwide, but we have chosen names mostly inspired by Anglo-Saxon traditions. Our moon names honour the whole lunar cycle, rather than just its fullest phase. Although we have included one moon per month, this is a simplification, as in reality the lunar cycles do not align neatly with the calendar months and will usually begin or end during the month on either side. It's also important to note that every few years there is an additional, thirteenth lunar cycle: we call this the Liminal moon and allocate it to the closest cycle to Samhain, usually between the Hunter's moon and the Frost moon.

Guiding words and seasonal symbols

We have given each month a guiding word, to offer an immediate sense of its feel and provide a focus for tasks or reflections. These words are accompanied by a seasonal symbol (something in nature that captures a key feeling of each month, such as falling leaves in November), the imagery of which adds a visual anchor and depth of meaning.

YOUR SACRED SPACE

In many nature-inspired traditions, especially those that explore the relationship between the wild worlds around and within us, it's considered important to have a physical space where that sense of connection to the seasons and the self can be honoured.

Some call it an altar, while others know it as a nature table; we call it a sacred space. The name doesn't matter, as long as it offers you somewhere to create a tangible expression of your inner and outer landscapes. It could be a shelf, a windowsill, or a box you pack away – choose whatever works best for you.

Throughout the book, as we explore each monthly archetype, we will invite you to add something to your sacred space to represent that part of yourself. Consider using items such as tarot or oracle cards, stones, leaves, feathers, shells, candles, photographs, poems, drawings, or personal objects. We also encourage you to add other foraged treasures as the seasons progress, to capture a sense of the changing year.

NOTES ON TERMINOLOGY

The Term 'Celtic'

Many sources of nature-inspired wisdom draw heavily on the idea of certain customs or practices with Celtic origins, loosely referencing the ancient tribal groups living in western and central Europe during the period spanning 700 BCE to 400 CE. However, the term is sometimes used inauthentically or incorrectly and is considered overly reductive by many modern archaeologists. As such, although you'll find that we do occasionally describe various (often mythological) ideas as 'Celtic' for ease, it's a label we hold lightly in our work.

Solar and Lunar Energy

Throughout the book you will encounter references to what we describe as solar and lunar energy. You might notice similarities here with the more commonly used concept of 'masculine' and 'feminine' ways of being, but we prefer to tune in to the qualities of the sun and moon, rather than reducing qualities shared by all humans to gendered stereotypes. In simple terms, our solar energy is connected with strength, power, focus, logic, order, and life force, while lunar energy is associated with reflection, emotion, intuition, healing, change, and the interconnected spiral of life. As with everything in the book, you are encouraged to consider your own versions of and relationship with solar and lunar energy.

TIME TO BEGIN YOUR JOURNEY

If you're ready to rewild, we invite you to take your first step and turn the page...

WINTER

EARTH | MIDNIGHT | FOREST | SAGE

As the foundational season of nature's annual cycle, winter is a time of deep inward exploration before the energy of the year begins to rise. Grounded symbolically in the stability of the Earth element, the quiet mystery of midnight, the tangled roots and winding paths of the forest soulscape, and the gentle wisdom of the Sage archetype, it offers a safe cocoon for germination and metamorphosis beneath the surface.

Winter invites us to see in the dark: to seek the truth of who we are and what we desire, and to cultivate the trust that's needed to await the return of the light. Whether welcomed or endured, these fallow months when the land lies bare offer a vital opportunity to rest, reflect, and renew in preparation for new growth yet to come.

NOVEMBER

ROOT

Preceded by the threshold of Samhain (Halloween) on the last day of October, November is the first month in the Wheel of the Year and signals the gradual transition into winter. As trees shed their leaves and we welcome the symbolic wisdom of the Earth element and the forest soulscape, this month encourages us to **root**: to slow our pace where we can, turn our attention inwards, and consider what feels meaningful and important in our lives as we begin the journey through another year. Supported by the grounding wisdom of the Sage archetype, this month is a good time to sit with questions of values and purpose, embracing the potent transformative nature of this seasonal shift to guide the descent into the dreaming space of midwinter.

THE ELDER TREE

The elder (*Sambucus*) stretches out its boned branches, beckoning you closer. In late spring or early summer, its frothy, cream flowers give the appearance of maiden-like vivacity and beauty, but do not be fooled, for this is the witches' tree. In winter, the youthful façade is stripped away, revealing the stark silhouette beneath: in this incarnation, the elder's skeletal twigs – brittle and worn – create the illusion of a stooped old woman, whose outward form contradicts her potent wisdom and magic.

While we may describe this figure as a 'witch', it is essential not to misunderstand this name. Despite the word's common associations with evil and harm, we must remember that this is a misinterpretation that arose through the persecution of 'cunning folk' which swept across the British Isles, Europe, and parts of North America during the 16th to 18th centuries. The elder tree empowers us to reclaim the true identity of the witch, as a revered knowledge-keeper and healer from whom insight and solace is sought.

THE ELDER TREE EMPOWERS US TO RECLAIM THE TRUE IDENTITY OF THE WITCH.

This gift for healing, in particular, is symbolised by the elder's fruit. Emerging first as small, hard beads with a green-red tinge, before plumping into deep purple spheres, elderberries can be transformed into a powerful immune-boosting tonic that helps stave off winter illness. Beyond nurturing the body, the elder's healing qualities also extend to the mind and soul, encouraging us to make peace with emotional darkness and seek out health and wholeness.

Like the fairytale witch of the woods, often described derisively as a 'crone' or 'hag', the elder tree is equally associated with old age. While ageing is generally viewed by mainstream culture as a descent into a 'lesser' phase of life, the elder inspires us to reframe the journey towards elderhood as a process of wild becoming; an initiation into untamed experience. Time holds no bounds for this tree, which recovers easily from damage and stands stalwart in winter landscapes, instilling us with strength and regenerative possibility. The elder reminds us that our souls come alive when we connect with the elements and the earth, feeling the pull of ancestral roots beneath our feet, which hold us safely and steadily in place.

Make an Ogham Stick

Carry the protective wisdom of the elder with you always by creating an Ogham stick (or wand, if you prefer). In the Ogham alphabet, the elder is represented by the letter 'ruis' (pronounced 'roo-esh') and denoted by the *symbol* ᚏ.

Sustainably source a small elder branch (or you could inscribe another wood or a stone) and, using paint or a pen, or even by carving, make the mark of the elder/ruis symbol. Keep this symbolic token in your pocket or by your bedside as a reminder of your inner wise self and the transformative power of the elder tree.

Elderberry Tea

Honour the spirit of the elder by drinking elderberry tea, which can be found in health food stores. If you wish, enrich your experience with a short tea meditation, by mindfully choosing your mug, noticing the scent of the elderberry and how the warming liquid feels on your lips, then tuning in to the sensation of tasting and drinking the tea.

THE FROST MOON

Named for the glittering shrouds of ice that can envelop landscapes on cold days, November's Frost lunar cycle offers a gentle reminder that winter's chill is creeping in. Although you may not experience frost at this time where you are, whether due to geographical location or the impact of climate change, the image remains a helpful invitation to consider how best to prepare for winter on a psychological level.

The Frost moon's arrival inspires us to ask ourselves what we might need to stay warm and nourished through the incoming colder months, and how we might tend to those needs from day to day. It's a prompt to establish or return to small rituals that keep our inner spark alive, whether that be lighting a candle at breakfast, cooking or baking with comforting spices, or wrapping up in cosy sweaters, scarves, and blankets.

In metaphorical terms, the tiny crystals and fractal patterns contained within veils of frost also remind us to pay close attention to the finer details of life, asking ourselves who and what matters most, and where we want to direct our energy as we begin a new yearly cycle. The transitional quality of frozen water holds hidden meaning, too, with its change in state from liquid to solid mirroring the wider shift from the swirling, watery depths of autumn to winter's grounded earth. This hints at the season's transformative potential: an enticing opportunity for being and becoming.

Ground Yourself

Have you ever tried grounding? Also known as earthing, this is a therapeutic technique that is said to realign the body's electrical energy through direct contact with the earth. The simplest way to do this is by standing barefoot on the ground outside – although this might sound unappealing at first, it can be an invigorating way to begin a frosty winter morning! Either as a one-off experience or part of a regular practice, taking time to root into the land with your feet on grass or soil can be deeply calming and connecting.

Seeking Wisdom from the Frost Moon

What in your life feels sparkling and precious?

How do you want to prepare for the winter months?

What meaningful patterns are present in your life?

What feels veiled or hidden right now?

What small details do you want to focus on this season?

In what way are you moving from one state of being to another?

THE SHAPESHIFTER

The first of three personas contained within winter's overarching Sage archetype, the Shapeshifter acts as a bridge between seasons, connecting the fluidity of autumn with the rootedness of winter. As a transitional period that marks the end of one cycle and the beginning of another, November is a month of flux: dreams for the year ahead are taking shape but not yet fully formed, and our sense of who we are may be equally unclear. We're called to reflect and release, and to invite in the vision of who we want to become.

Winter is a season of darkness, not just of the season but of the self. It's a natural time to delve into the depths of the inner world: a cauldron of creativity and imagination, but also a resting place for the old bones or raw realities of carefully cradled griefs and losses. These encounters can be as hard as they are healing and, acting as a soul guide to the Underworld, the Shapeshifter holds our hands and hearts as we edge into the shadowlands of winter, supporting the dissolution of identity in pursuit of truth, while knowing that wholeness waits on the other side.

Myths and folktales offer many examples of the Shapeshifter, often with a sinister undertone. The Morrígan, the Irish 'phantom queen' of war and fate, appeared as a crow and was thought to foretell death, as well as victory, in battle. In Scottish culture, Beira, queen of winter, who takes the form of a rock throughout spring and summer, was said to come alive at Samhain and use her power to unleash cold and darkness, while kelpies (water horses) and selkies (seal folk) could take the form of beautiful women who would lure unsuspecting men to untimely ends. Cerridwen, the Welsh medieval enchantress, turned into a dog, an otter, a hawk, and a hen when hunting down a boy who mistakenly consumed an elixir of knowledge intended for her son.

However, there are alternative readings of many of these tales which reverse their narratives and portray shapeshifters as complex and misunderstood. Though frequently fierce, they are also often revealed to be sensitive, empathic creatures who are feared and persecuted for their otherness or tricked and exploited for their magic. In life as in myth, it is vital to embrace the shadows, grey areas, and tender places within ourselves, so we might feel more deeply and become more wholeheartedly alive.

The Shapeshifting Self

Write down all the ways in which you are a shapeshifter: changeable, inconsistent, complicated. How does it feel to acknowledge these parts of yourself? Is it uncomfortable or reassuring? How can you become more fully yourself by honouring all your forms?

YOUR SACRED SPACE

Choose a symbol for your inner Shapeshifter to add to your sacred space, such as a feather, a fallen leaf, or a list of words describing all the parts of yourself. (You can find out more about this practice in the Introduction.) What do you think best reflects this fluctuating aspect of your identity?

THE STARLING

The shapeshifters of the wild world, starlings flock in murmurations: huge, swirling groups that peak in the winter months and can include anywhere from tens of thousands to millions of birds, all moving in unison as though guided by some subliminal connection or invisible force. The reasons for these aerial displays, which appear as fluid, cloud-like forms in the sky, are largely a mystery, but are thought to offer an element of protection against the attacks of birds of prey; a behaviour that perfectly captures the Shapeshifter's evasive nature.

Elusiveness is something that comes through in their song, too, which includes varied sounds often copied not only from other birds, but also from humans or machines – a deception that can cause uneasiness and confusion. This gift for mimicry features in the *The Mabinogion*, a medieval anthology of early Welsh legends, while Mozart was said to have kept a pet starling who could sing phrases from his compositions. As boisterous birds unafraid to use their voice, starlings symbolise the Shapeshifter's commitment to self-expression.

Alongside their trickster tendencies, starlings also reflect the magic of the Shapeshifter in their physical appearance. With a cloak of dark feathers tinged with shimmering purple and green, and flecks of silver that almost look like tiny stars, these fascinating birds have a spellbinding quality that makes them as alluring as a selkie's song.

Swirling Skies

Seek out a starling murmuration to enjoy a truly magical experience. If you're able to go in person, research where they tend to take place near you (usually over marshes or open fields with nearby woodland, but sometimes in urban areas too) and aim to arrive at the location at dusk, around an hour before sunset. Otherwise, there are lots of clips online that will give you a sense of this captivating phenomenon.

FALLING LEAVES

As autumn gives way to winter, the leaves of deciduous trees fall to the earth, carpeting the landscape with shades of yellow and gold, scarlet and burgundy. This annual release occurs when trees produce less of the hormone auxin as the temperature cools, and the bond between leaves and their branches weakens and then finally breaks.

Losing their leaves enables trees to expend less energy during the winter season, and instead they can conserve water to prevent the trunk from drying out. Additionally, with the leaves gone, strong winds can blow through the branches, which helps the tree bend with the weather, rather than fighting against it. And of course, the fallen leaves serve their purpose too, composting down into the earth and nourishing the roots.

The falling leaves this month invite us to likewise shed what no longer serves us, to let go of any feelings, responses, or actions that have no place in our future. In this process, rather than simply discarding all these things, we can acknowledge their presence and the ways in which they have shaped our life, before choosing to 'compost' them within, nurturing our inner 'soil' and preparing for future growth. Just like deciduous trees, we too can gain strength from moving and flowing with nature rather than against it.

Release Ritual

Create a ritual around this practice of letting go. Forage for a collection of medium to large fallen leaves that you feel drawn to, making sure to gather them on a dry day.

Using a non-toxic pen, write directly onto the leaves all the things you want to let go of and compost.

You can then choose to bury them in the soil, make a mandala (a pattern on the ground), burn them on a bonfire, float them on a river, or simply let them fly free into the wind.

DECEMBER

RENEW

December is the month of midwinter, but with the arrival of the Winter Solstice there is also a sense of rebirth, as the sun stands still for a moment in time before leading us into the waxing half of the year. At this time, we are called to **renew**, a word that invites restoration and the return of new life or strength. This sense of renewal mirrors the movements of the wild world at this time of year: although landscapes can appear bare, stripped back, and sometimes devoid of life, beneath the surface there is a gentle rekindling of energy beginning to take place. Winter's influence will remain strong for a while yet, but the approach of a new calendar year invites us to consider what is stirring deep within. Nourishment is crucial, and throughout this month we are reminded to find a steady rhythm that sustains the mind and body through the cold and dark.

THE BIRCH TREE

Enter a birch forest, and you will find all eyes on you. These 'eyes' – distinctive marks that appear on the trunk of birch trees – are formed when branches die and fall from the tree, leaving only the outline of their original connection point behind. These imprinted memories remind us to honour our own 'fallen branches' in the same way, by pausing to recognise all that we have released and composted over the autumn months.

The birch (*Betula*), and in particular the silver birch (*Betula pendula*), is known for shedding its bark as part of its natural growth cycle, representing another invitation for us to let go of old layers. At the same time, the eyes of the birch symbolise clarity and foresight, calling on us to look ahead and embrace the fresh new surface forming underneath. In pagan and Nordic traditions, the birch is often used to make twig brooms, which are used at the year's end to sweep out stagnant energy and unwelcome spirits; cleansing the home through simultaneous release and renewal.

Alongside this inner wisdom, the birch also offers practical support, with its peeling skin once having been used as 'paper' for writing. In prehistoric times, birch bark was also used to make a kind of tar, enabling Palaeolithic humans to glue items together. Additionally, there is a special type of fungi that grows on birch trees; birch polypore (*Fomitopsis betulina*) can be used as tinder to light fires, and has also been turned to as a form of medicine over time. Famously, the body of Ötzi, found in the Alps in 1991, over 5,000 years after his death, was discovered with pieces of birch polypore, thought to have been carried as an antiseptic in case of injury. Inspired by these pragmatic uses, the birch can encourage our own consideration of what resources we may need at this time.

Start Anew

Sweep the old year out of the door at the Winter Solstice (or New Year's Eve), using a sweeping brush or broom. Traditionally, this practice would have dispelled any unwanted spirits lingering in the home, while also creating space for renewal and beginning afresh.

Seeking a Word for the Year

As we turn the page on the calendar year, many of us are thinking of the months and seasons that lie ahead. Rather than getting caught up in the hustle and pressure that often arise at this time, choose instead to pause intentionally, perhaps completing this activity around the time of the Winter Solstice.

On a piece of paper, draw or paint (or use charcoal if you have some) the 'eye' of a birch tree. In the centre of this eye, write down a word or phrase that you would like to act as a guide for the year ahead. Pin this onto a bulletin board, your fridge, or in your planner. Return to it regularly.

THE OAK MOON

On the surface, 'Oak' may seem a strange choice of name for this lunar cycle, for in winter the oak is stripped of its leaves, skeletal and bare, presenting an entirely different silhouette to its full green canopy at the height of summer. Yet the continued strength of its trunk and branches offers an important reminder that if we pare back and focus our energy, we too can stay resilient amid the darkness of midwinter.

Oak is known in pagan circles as *duir* (pronounced 'dure') – the seventh letter of the Ogham tree alphabet – and it's said that this early Irish word could have evolved from the Sanskrit root *dwr*, meaning 'door'. Emphasised by the fact that many doors were traditionally crafted from oak due to its great strength (*duir* is the likely origin of the word 'durable'), the oak tree is symbolically connected to the idea of doorways and thresholds. At the Winter Solstice, it represents the 'doorway' to the waxing half of the year, as the sun prepares to be reborn.

At this point, it is said that the Oak King reclaims his crown from the Holly King, who has reigned over the earth for six months since the Summer Solstice back in June, when the oak was at the height of its full resplendent growth. The Oak King regaining control once again in December symbolises the gradual shift back towards the lighter months of the year, as the days begin to lengthen and the power of the sun returns.

Note: You can read more about the symbolism and arboreal wisdom of the oak in the summer section, where it features as our guiding tree for the month of June.

The Light Returns

Honour the story of the Oak King and the Holly King by carrying a sprig of holly to an oak tree and leaving it as an offering by its roots, as a symbol of the transition of power and the anticipated return of the oak's greenery. As you leave your offering, give thanks for all that has sustained you over the past six months as the sunlight and the year has waned, and remember the hope that the Oak King offers as the energy of the earth now slowly returns.

Seeking Wisdom from the Oak Moon

Thinking back to last June, what has flourished or faded over the past six months?

Where do you want to direct your energy this month?

What helps you to feel strong and powerful?

What rituals might help you to stay resilient through midwinter?

As we mark the rebirth of the sun, in what ways do you feel ready to welcome renewal?

What are you hopeful for in the coming months?

THE PHILOSOPHER

Having now moved into the heart of winter, where the influence of the Earth element is at its peak, the Philosopher represents a more solid, grounded form of the season's overarching Sage archetype than November's fluctuating Shapeshifter. Representing knowledge and experience, the Philosopher – like the Oak moon – helps us to stand strong and true in the face of hardships, whether in the sense of facing December's outward cold and dark or navigating the inner challenges of an emotional 'winter'.

That being said, alongside this sturdy support coexists the important ability to sit with questions rather than simply rushing to seek answers. Guided by the theme of renewal, midwinter is a time for the creative imagining that comes before tangible action, as well as the rest and replenishment that precedes the growth of spring. With this in mind, the Philosopher encourages us to explore existential themes of meaning and purpose, and to cultivate the trust (or perhaps even faith) required to weather periods of stagnancy or uncertainty.

As the Winter Solstice marks both the darkest day of the year (death or old age) *and* the turning point back towards the light (life or youth), the Philosopher represents both the wisdom of elderhood and the curiosity of childhood. Weaving both of these together allows this archetype to hold us steady with a mature perspective anchored in past experience, while also inspiring us to hope and dream for the future with childlike wonder.

Your Guiding Principles

Consider your 'philosophy' for life. What is important to you? What questions kindle your curiosity and shape your desire to learn? Inspired by the Philosopher archetype, take some time to think about the foundational beliefs that inform your understanding of yourself and the world, and note down your reflections as a manifesto to guide your onward journey through the year.

YOUR SACRED SPACE

What could you add to your sacred space to represent the quietly questioning Philosopher? Suggestions include a book, your guiding principles (see left), or a photograph of an inspiring elder-figure.

THE PHILOSOPHER ENCOURAGES US TO EXPLORE EXISTENTIAL THEMES OF MEANING AND PURPOSE.

THE OWL

Nocturnal and intelligent, owls have long been revered as mysterious, shadowy symbols of deep knowing. The little owl was the trusted companion of Athena, the ancient Greek goddess of wisdom (and her Roman counterpart, Minerva) – a connection that potentially filtered into the Latin name for the little owl, *Athene noctua*, a name which is still used scientifically today. The Romans were also said to practise ornithomancy, which is the art of divining the future by observing and interpreting the calls and flight patterns of birds. The behaviour of owls was respected as a particularly powerful form of prophecy, alongside that of ravens, crows, eagles, and vultures.

In Scottish and Irish culture, the owl is associated with the Cailleach: 'the veiled one'. She is a formidable crone figure of great influence and insight, whose power is drawn from and exerted over the elements and the land, particularly harsher weathers and terrains such as snow, wind, rain, and rock. Very much a persona of winter, the Cailleach is connected with elderhood, death and rebirth, knowledge, and foresight – all of which are also themes of the owl, which is sometimes known by the traditional name of *cailleach oidhche* (Scots Gaelic) or *cailleach oíche* (Irish), meaning 'night hag'.

The barn owl (*Tyto alba*) captures the spirit of the Philosopher archetype. Keen-eyed, sharp of hearing, and able to turn its head 180 degrees in either direction, it has the same depth of perception, holistic perspective, and clear-sighted vision for the future. With a lightweight body carried by expansive, soft-feathered wings, the barn owl's ability to fly slowly and quietly, gliding almost silently through the night, also reflects the Philosopher's gentle, considered nature and the idea of easing gradually through the remainder of winter.

The Bones of the Year

After consuming their prey, owls leave the inedible remains as pellets: small, oval-shaped bundles of fur and bones. December, and midwinter in general, is a 'skeletal' time of year: bare tree branches stand stark against the sky, the dark nights are associated with death, and the chill in the air can creep right to the core. Here, at the renewal point of the Winter Solstice, consider the 'bones' of the previous 12 months. If your life were an owl pellet, what memories, experiences, or learnings would you find within it? Write down your reflections as a way of honouring the old before embracing the new.

EVERGREENS

Now the falling leaves of November are behind us, scattered across pavements and pathways, clustered in damp piles, or forming winter homes for hibernating animals, in December the wild world can seem quite bleak. But if you look in the right places, there is always hope and life to be found.

In contrast to deciduous trees, evergreen foliage remains green throughout the year, providing a permanent and reassuring presence in gardens and woodlands and symbolising everlasting life amid the darkness and cold of midwinter. And remember the Holly King? Perhaps as a final farewell, but also as a means of protection against unwanted spirits, the holly's evergreen spikes would traditionally have adorned houses at this time of year. Ivy, yew, and pine were also popular decorations, often seen alongside candles to represent the sun's light and rejoice in its return.

Today, Christmas traditions may have merged with or overtaken those of the Winter Solstice, but the nature-inspired roots of many festive customs remain interwoven with the modern-day approach. To appreciate the darkness around you when it feels cold and perhaps a little melancholy can often be a difficult task, but as we face the light and a new beginning, remember that the symbolic hope of evergreens can sustain you during the depths of midwinter.

Symbolic Evergreens

Create an evergreen crown or table display. For the crown use a base of thin, flexible branches, or use ribbon or twine, and for the table display, you can follow your creativity!

Weave in some evergreens that feel symbolic for this point in your personal journey. Choose ivy for faithfulness and life force; yew for regeneration and rebirth; pine for healing and purification; or fir for endurance and hope.

JANUARY

SEEK

As the final full month of winter, January brings a subtle shift in energy. The cold and darkness continue, reminding us to maintain a slow approach where we can, but, having passed the shortest day back in December, we know the light is now gradually returning. Hazel catkins and early blooms such as winter aconites begin to appear in woodlands, and prints left on frosty ground show which birds and animals are becoming more active. The first day of the month signals the resetting of the calendar year and a societal rush towards the promise of new beginnings, while nature's rhythm encourages us to welcome this sense of hope on our own terms, rejecting frantic goal setting in favour of gentle dreaming. Our guiding word for this phase is **seek**: an invitation to consider our desires and craft a rich and intentional vision for the year ahead.

THE ROWAN TREE

In January we may be tentatively taking our first steps into the new calendar year, but the nebulous nature of midwinter can mean that our visions and ideas for the months ahead still feel fragile and fragmented. The entrance of the rowan (*Sorbus*), a tree of protection, is much needed at this time, holding themes of healing, health, and wholeness.

The bright, red-orange berries of the rowan tree, which appear in early autumn, display on their base the pattern of a pentagram – the five-pointed star that is a meaningful symbol in many different spiritual traditions. Within pagan-inspired beliefs, the pentagram represents the five elements (Earth, Air, Fire, Water, Aether) and the interconnection of all life, and this symbolism - alongside the rowan's association with safety and wellness - perhaps inspired the tradition of planting these trees near doorways and stone circles, and in cemeteries, as a means of warding off evil spirits.

Alongside these more ephemeral, magical qualities, the rowan is also known as a tree of strength. Although it can grow in lowlands, it more commonly appears in mountainous areas (its alternative name is mountain ash) – an indication of its hardy character and a reminder that we, too, have the resilience to overcome challenging circumstances. Amid the bleakness of midwinter, the rowan inspires this gathering of strength, as well as care for self, each other, and the wild world.

Protecting What You Seek

Although our dreams and visions for the year ahead may feel fragile right now, the rowan can protect these soft new shoots until spring arrives. Draw your own pentagram shape and see each of the five points as representing an element. Now, using these elements as a guide, explore what it is you are seeking, either right now, or in the months or year ahead. You can use the suggested guiding questions below if helpful.

- **Earth:** What are you seeking that will help you feel grounded, rooted, and stable?
- **Air:** What are you seeking that will bring more space and freedom to your life?
- **Fire:** What are you seeking that will help you feel more alive?
- **Water:** What are you seeking that will help you to feel more in flow?
- **Aether:** Intuitively, what one word sums up what you are seeking?

Note a brief response next to each point of the star, before drawing a circle to enclose the star and your words to protect what it is you are seeking.

Your Inner Resilience

Find something that symbolises the resilience and protection of the rowan for you. It might be an item with an inscribed pentagram, a small stone, a rowan leaf, a piece of bark, or something personally meaningful. Place the object in your pocket or bag, or in your sacred space, and come back to it whenever you need reminding of your inner strength.

THE WOLF MOON

According to the *Anglo-Saxon Chronicle*, a collection of Old English historical records, January was once known as Wolf Monath (wolf month) as it marked the beginning of wolf-hunting season among the nobility. Sadly, this kind of persecution ultimately drove wolves to extinction across Britain, but the echoes of their haunting winter howls remain present in the first lunar cycle of the calendar year.

Wolves have long been associated with winter: the Swedish expression *vargavinter* (wolf winter) describes a prolonged period of harsh weather, while Norse mythology proclaimed that the legendary wolf Sköll would one day devour the sun at the coming of *fimbulvetr*, the Great Winter. With these ideas in mind, the Wolf moon encourages us to hold steady in the face of January's societal push out of hibernation, reminding us that winter is not yet over and a cautious emergence is key.

Given that wolves are known for their wild instinct, the Wolf moon also indicates that late winter remains a time of introspection, when we're called to draw on our intuition. For wolves, this instinctive knowing is deeply connected to hunting, meaning they represent not only the pull towards seeking or visioning that often arises in January, but also the endurance needed to travel through the remainder of winter.

Though wolves are often presented as solitary predators, they are, in fact, incredibly sociable creatures who live in packs and can be associated with community and loyalty. Contrary to common misinterpretations, 'lone wolves' tend only to have separated from their group in order to find new territory, seek out a mate, or start a new pack. These wolves are known as 'dispersers' and can be thought of as a symbol of the pioneering spirit and hope for the future that often feels so present in January.

Use Your Wolf Voice

Listen to a clip of a wolf howling (there are plenty online) and notice how it makes you feel in your mind and body. Then, if you're curious and courageous enough to give it a go, find a quiet place where you won't be disturbed – either in your home or, even better, out in the wild – and try howling as loud as you feel able to. It may seem strange at first but see if you can let go of any censoring or judgement and allow yourself to express and release whatever it is you're holding inside through the sound of your voice. You can do it with a friend or in a group if that will help! If you want to go all-in on the experience, see if you can plan it to coincide with the full Wolf moon.

Seeking Wisdom from the Wolf Moon

What parts of yourself have been misunderstood or driven away?

In what ways have you experienced a 'vargavinter' (a harsh or difficult period) in recent times?

What message does your intuition have for you this season and how is it making itself known?

What are you hunting or seeking this winter or this year?

How might the theme of endurance apply to your current circumstances?

In what ways do you find comfort with the pack, and in what ways are you a solo pioneer?

THE VISIONARY

This month, the questioning Philosopher archetype of December is replaced by the Visionary: the part of self who seeks answers and longs to start bringing dreams to life through big-picture planning. The word 'vision' refers to the ability to see, and we can think of this facet of winter's wider Sage archetype as our inner seer and guide: a source of insight and direction.

The Visionary emerges from December's focus on renewal, bringing light to the darkness of late winter and illuminating the hazy corners of our minds. Without pulling us frantically into January's typical pressure and pace, this rising clarity offers a glimmer of energy and possibility that helps us shake off the slumber of hibernation and start mapping out the year ahead.

Fittingly, the term 'visionary' describes not only those blessed with clear sight and keen perception, but also the gift of richly detailed and imaginative thinking. When the idea of new beginnings is so alive in us from a societal perspective, it can be energising to embrace this sense of creative potential to move beyond fear or uncertainty and boldly claim the vision toward which we're moving.

It's important to note, however, that seeing is not the same as doing: the Visionary understands that January is still very much a winter month, and that there is no need to rush into definitive action before we're ready. This is a phase for gentle inner searching, safe in the knowledge that taking time to 'see in the dark' now will help us move forward more confidently once spring arrives.

THE VISIONARY: THE PART OF SELF WHO SEEKS ANSWERS AND LONGS TO START BRINGING DREAMS TO LIFE.

Make a Vision Board

Make a vision board for the new calendar year. Get clear on everything that feels important over the next 12 months (whether things that are already part of your life or those you're still working towards) and visually represent them by cutting out words and images from old magazines to make a collage (or create a digital version if you prefer). Keep your vision board somewhere you can see it every day, such as on a bulletin board or as a screensaver.

YOUR SACRED SPACE

What could you add to your sacred space to represent the illuminating, imaginative Visionary? Suggestions include a star symbol, a depiction of a wolf, or your vision board.

THE WOLF

As 'the month of the wolf', there can only be one choice for January's animal guide. The Cailleach (the elemental crone of winter, who we met in December's chapter) is often portrayed riding on a wolf to emphasise her connection with wild spirit, and these beautiful animals offer a potent reminder of the wildness we all hold within. At the same time, their narrative shows that it's not always easy or safe to embrace this part of self: like the witches and cunning folk persecuted throughout history for their untamed nature, wolves have been equally feared and hunted.

As humans, our relationship with the wolf – and with wildness itself – can be complex. On the one hand, we are drawn to the wolf's association with freedom and intuition, and the kinship of the pack, and on the other we are deeply afraid of something we perhaps don't quite understand. Much like the darkness of winter, wolves are mysterious in ways that can be both alluring and frightening. This twilight quality has earned the wolf a strong association with the psychological concept of the Shadow – the hidden underbelly of the psyche.

In ancient Greek mythology wolves were known as tricksters and outsiders, in Roman culture as keepers of power, and in Norse tradition as an emblem of both loyalty and chaos. In Old English the word *wulf* also meant 'devil', and stories of dangerous night-prowlers (from the Wulver of Scottish folklore to the fairytale Big Bad Wolf) have filtered into our consciousness, subtly shaping our perceptions. Is it any wonder we're wary of our wildness, when the myth of the werewolf's monthly transformation has villainised our innate capacity for cyclical change?

In those areas of the world where wolves survive, they are regarded as a keystone species – meaning they help to shape the ecosystems around them in fundamental ways. Applying this to our inner landscape encourages us to hold our own wolf-self close, knowing it can help us find and follow our wild instincts as the year unfolds.

Your Wild Wolf-Self

Spend some time thinking of all the ways you might believe that wolves and wildness are 'bad' or threatening, then consider how these ideas might be holding you back from fully knowing and embracing your wild self. How could you 'be more wolf' this winter and beyond?

THE NORTH STAR

Glimmering in the inky night, the North Star lights the way for us as the dream-like season of winter comes to a close. Marking due north, it appears to hold still in the sky, while everything else turns around it. It is not the brightest star, but it is easy to spot, and as such acts as a waymarker for many nocturnal travellers.

Currently, the North Star in our skies is Polaris, but travel back 5,000 years and Thuban, a much dimmer star, held the title due to the shift of the earth's rotational axis. It will be another 13,000 years before Polaris hands over its reign to the star Vega, and its longevity as our midnight guide invites considerations of deep time and all our ancestors – both human and more-than-human – who may have sought solace in its light.

As we prepare to emerge from midwinter, the North Star represents our trusted inner compass, guiding us to connect with our own sense of direction and self as we move steadily and surely towards our dreams and visions.

Find Your Guiding Star

Gather words and phrases that represent your dreams for the year ahead, and the feelings or values you want to hold onto – perhaps turning to your vision board for guidance. Note them down on paper, imagining each word or phrase as a star. Think carefully about sizing: make the most important ideas larger and the more secondary themes smaller. Whichever word or phrase is the biggest is your north star – an intention or feeling that you want to prioritise above all else.

Once you have noted down all your words, think about the relationships and connections between them. Which ideas are intertwined with others? You might like to draw lines to link these 'stars', creating an interconnected constellation depicting your overall vision.

SPRING

AIR | DAWN | MOUNTAIN | MAIDEN

We welcome spring with the anticipation of rising energy. As the season turns and we leave behind the rooted stillness of winter, we embrace a new set of associations: the freedom and expansion of the Air element, the soft morning light of dawn, the adventure and perspective of the mountain soulscape, and the playful curiosity of the Maiden archetype.

With spring's arrival, the wild world awakens from her slumber and we too are called to shift our attention from inward reflection to outward connection, seeking opportunities to rekindle feelings of community and togetherness. Supported by the stirring of life around us, we experience a gradual movement towards growth, tending to the fresh green shoots of plans and ideas as they surface from within.

FEBRUARY

EMERGE

After the depths of winter, February's arrival guides us into the quickening of the year. Imbolc (pronounced 'im-olk') comes from Old Irish and means 'in the belly'. Its celebration on the first of the month signals the onset of lambing season and the growing potential of the fertile earth. As an early spring fire festival, Imbolc releases the hold of winter and welcomes in a new kind of gently pulsating energy and life force. This is a time of tentative unfurling, of easing slowly out of winter hibernation, taking care to protect the seeds and tender new shoots of the wild world and of self. It will soon lead us to a more dynamic phase of change and growth, but for now we are guided to **emerge:** to reach out our tendrils and embrace the soft morning light.

THE WILLOW TREE

There is an ancient Druidic tale that the universe was born from two eggs hidden in a willow tree. One egg contained the sun and the other contained the earth, and as they hatched, the cosmos was born. Unsurprisingly, then, the willow (*Salix*) is the first tree of spring, symbolic of emerging life and new beginnings. This process of emergence, though welcome, is often also laced with sadness or difficulty. It marks a more final letting go of everything shed back in early winter, as the trappings and fragments of this previous season, this old self, are blown away by the winds of spring to make space for new growth.

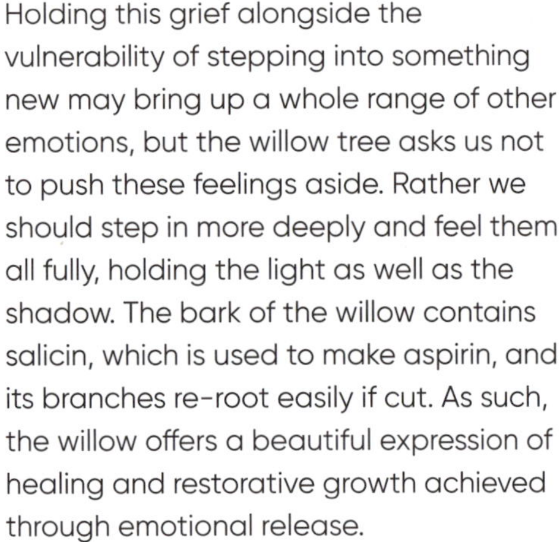

Holding this grief alongside the vulnerability of stepping into something new may bring up a whole range of other emotions, but the willow tree asks us not to push these feelings aside. Rather we should step in more deeply and feel them all fully, holding the light as well as the shadow. The bark of the willow contains salicin, which is used to make aspirin, and its branches re-root easily if cut. As such, the willow offers a beautiful expression of healing and restorative growth achieved through emotional release.

Although the willow is a spring tree symbolically, connected to the Air element and its themes of expansion and freedom, it is also a tree that thrives in watery locations. This connection to water – the element of autumn and spring's opposing partner – reminds us that we can turn to our inner depths and flow of emotions to help us navigate a time of year that can sometimes be overwhelming in its wakening pace. We can hold space for reflection and gentleness alongside the rising energy of the season.

Note: There are many species of willow, but the symbolism explored here comes mostly from the white willow (*Salix alba*).

THE WILLOW OFFERS A BEAUTIFUL EXPRESSION OF HEALING AND RESTORATIVE GROWTH.

Willow Wisdom

Flexible and easily pliable, the willow is adaptable to change. As we navigate this seasonal transition, consider how you might act as the willow when you are presented with change; what do you need to feel held and supported during these phases? Note down a phrase of guidance or affirmation in your journal, on your phone background, or on your fridge, written as a message from the willow tree. Turn to these words as often as you need.

Tuning in to Your Emotions

Intentionally carve out space to connect with your feelings. That could be a regular journalling practice, pulling oracle or tarot cards each Monday (or moon day, associated with emotion), or simply asking yourself daily: *How do I feel?*

THE SNOW MOON

Although this month moves us away from midwinter, February weather tends to feel far from spring-like. Historically, it has often been the snowiest time of year, and traditional weather lore suggests that 'if February give much snow, a fine summer it doth foreshow'. In more recent years, snow has been thin on the ground in many regions due to the changing climate, but its symbolism remains a valuable reminder that, despite the seasonal shift, there is a need to pace ourselves at this time of year, to take things slowly as we emerge from hibernation.

The image of crisp, clean snow continues the 'fresh start' feeling that arrives in January with the new calendar year but tempers it with the sense of hushed quiet that a snow-covered landscape can bring. We are offered a blank canvas and an opportunity to begin again, but with pathways and landmarks covered; the way ahead isn't always clear. The Snow moon reminds us that sometimes setting out towards our visions can also mean setbacks, and tentative plans can melt like snowflakes when grasped too tightly.

Alongside this sense of caution, the symbolism of the Snow moon is also captured in the arrival of snowdrops. These beautiful, white flowers are often the first to nod their heads in late winter and early spring, offering a hopeful glimpse of the change that is beginning to unfold.

Nurturing Your 'Seeds'

Write down all the big ideas you have for things you want to do this year – these are your 'seeds'. They might be work-related, personal, feelings-based, or practical, and they will probably emerge from the ideas you cultivated and explored throughout the winter.

Now consider how you can continue to nurture each of these, so they are ready for planting once the snow has melted. What do they need to survive this phase? It might be time and space to plan them out more fully. It might be that some kind of gentle action is needed or you might simply need to remember that these are important to you. Think about and/or journal a response for each seed.

Seeking Wisdom from the Snow Moon

In what ways might you slow down right now?

How might you release your grasp and welcome the unknown?

How might you find more quiet and peace in your life?

In what ways are you feeling called to begin again?

If you quieten the noise of others, what is the one resounding message you want to hold close?

What is the change beginning to unfurl in your life?

THE INITIATE

Tipping from winter into early spring brings a shift in archetypal energy, as we leave behind the rooted energy of the Sage (our inner elder) and welcome the more spirited influence of the Maiden, our inner child. With the arrival of February, we encounter the first version of this new seasonal presence: the Initiate, or beginner.

To be initiated into something means to be introduced or inducted into a way of being, and this is essentially what happens during the earliest phase of spring, when we awaken from winter hibernation and learn how to engage with the world once more. We might be considering what we need in this cycle in order to thrive – perhaps adjusting rituals and routines or revisiting and refreshing old stories and beliefs – alongside welcoming any new hopes that have transpired from our winter dreaming. Although sometimes hesitant or even reluctant, the Initiate is curious and open and supports us as we start taking tangible steps forward on our path through the year.

Once this process is underway and the pace of spring's unfurling begins to quicken, the Initiate's focus shifts from the tentative and slightly passive stance of *being* initiated to the more confident and proactive role of *initiating:* taking control, making decisions, and facilitating growth. This paves the way for the bolder Maiden archetypes of March and April, who will lead us fully beyond the reach of winter and into the lighter months ahead.

A helpful figure to turn to for guidance at this time is the Irish goddess Brigid, a solar deity known as the bearer of an eternal flame, the keeper of the hearth or home fire, and patron of healing, inspiration, and craft. Reflecting the duality of the Initiate, she is sometimes imagined as a gentle fertility goddess who embodies the quiet potential of early spring, or as a sovereign warrior with a crown of light. Whatever her form, in February Brigid kindles the embers of winter into the spark of spring and encourages us to tend thoughtfully to our own inner flame.

The Flame of Initiation

For various reasons Brigid is associated with the number 19, and rituals dedicated to her around the time of Imbolc often extend over this many days.

To connect with your inner Initiate, find a long, white candle and, using a ruler and a pen, carefully make marks along its length at 19 equal intervals.

Either on the first day of February, or another day of your choosing, begin a short morning or evening practice of lighting the candle and letting it burn down to the next mark.

Do this every day for 19 days, spending the first nine days reflecting on all the ways you are currently being initiated (learning, renewing, receiving), the following nine days considering what you want to initiate (start) yourself, and the final day setting intentions for how you want to move forward.

YOUR SACRED SPACE

What could you add to your sacred space to represent the Initiate's focus on learning and beginning? Suggestions include a photograph of yourself as a child, a bulb or young plant, or a cutting from a willow tree.

THE DEER

Imagine a deer (or perhaps, more specifically, a doe) standing at the edge of a wood: half-hidden from view, ears pricked and listening intently, one hoof raised in readiness to move further into the open or retreat into the trees. This is how many of us feel in February, as we hesitate at the threshold between winter and spring. With caution, and perhaps some resistance, we seek to establish whether it's the right time to fully emerge or whether a longer period of rest or reflection would serve us better. Especially for those living in parts of the world where winter lingers well into March or even April, it can be difficult to connect with spring's rising energy as early as February.

Either way, what the deer symbolises above all is the gentleness required at this time of year – not only in terms of how we approach re-engaging with life after winter, but also when it comes to how we treat ourselves and others during this fragile phase of early growth. To support a transition into spring that feels uplifting rather than overwhelming, it's vital to tread carefully and slowly to avoid trampling tender new shoots or finding ourselves more exposed than we're ready for.

On the Cusp

On a piece of paper, draw a vertical line to create two parallel columns. Imagine you are the deer at the edge of the woods, with the line representing the threshold where the safety of the trees meets the wider world beyond.

In the left column (the woods), write down all the things that feel delicate or which you're not yet ready to reveal or share.

In the right column (the wider world), note down anything you feel confident to bring into the light.

How does seeing things this way make you feel and what might you need to do or change as a result?

SNOWDROPS

Heralded as one of the first flowers to bloom, snowdrops often feel quite miraculous and precious when they appear, as winter slackens its grip and we see emerging signs of renewal in the wild world. Symbolic of Imbolc, they are also connected to the Christian celebration of Candlemas (2nd February), and as a result are often known as Candlemas bells. Their nodding flower heads salt woodlands and cemeteries, and their hopeful, white flowers remind us of the waxing light of the solar year.

Despite their obvious connotations of hope, these delicate, milk-white flowers are also connected to darker themes. Once seen as an omen of death, in the Victorian era in particular it was deemed bad luck to pick snowdrops and bring them indoors, and doing so was said to bring misfortune on the family.

Today, this 'fair maid of February' offers a more positive reminder that when change feels impossible or out of reach, there are always stirrings beneath the surface and pockets of joy to be found.

Hope in the Darkness

To help you navigate this phase of the year, what might act as your symbol of hope? It might be an actual snowdrop, perhaps blooming in your garden or captured in a photograph pinned to your wall. Or it could be something completely different, something that will invite you to stay hopeful, no matter what life throws at you. Choose your symbol and then place it in your sacred space this month.

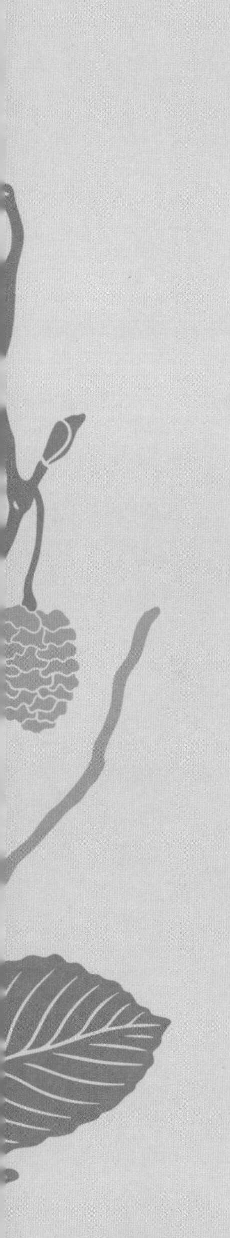

MARCH

EXPLORE

As the month of the Spring Equinox, March invites us to step fully into the heart of the season and allow ourselves to embrace the rising energy of the year. It is now that we really begin to notice the effects of the returning light, feeling a heightened sense of possibility and often experiencing a desire to re-engage with the wider world. March, which also heralds the renewal of the astrological year, can feel for many like the 'true beginning' of the cycle – a time of intuitive awakening, when the body becomes more able to hold and channel the increasing aliveness of the mind. Guided by curiosity and courage, during this phase we're called to **explore**: to reach upwards and outwards and start bringing plans to life with tangible action.

THE ALDER TREE

The Spring Equinox in March not only represents the peak of the season but also offers a rare moment of equilibrium in the natural world, when night and day are roughly equal in length. As such, it's a time associated with rejuvenation and balance – both of which are reflected within the alder (*Alnus*). Its spiralling buds symbolise the continual cycle of life, and its combination of male and female catkins means it radiates both solar and lunar energy.

Alder's gentle, lunar traits are reflected in its propensity to grow near water – the element most closely associated with emotion – as well as in the way its roots work with certain bacteria to enrich the soil with nitrogen, thereby nurturing and supporting neighbouring trees. Its more assertive solar side comes through in the physical substance of the tree itself: alder is a hardwood and was traditionally used to make shields, linking it to themes of protection and defence. Furthermore, as a water-seeking tree, its timber is resistant to the rot that can be caused by exposing wood to wet conditions, making it a symbol of strength and endurance.

The alder is also associated with Air, the element of spring: whistles can be made from its shoots, which are said to have once been used at this time of year to call upon the spirits of the wind. There's something magical about the notion of creating music from breath, and this sense of enchantment firmly connects the alder with the playful and mischievous world of the faerie folk. At the same time, if we think about breath as being vital to life, and song or spoken words as an expression of self, we can see that this is also a tree rooted firmly in human experience, which can inspire us to live fully and to share our authentic voice.

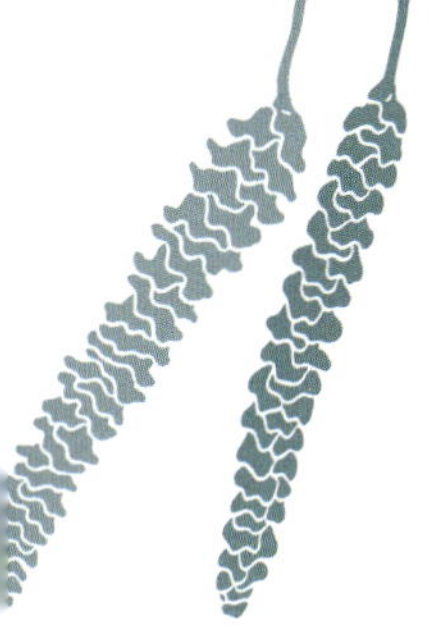

Take a Breath

To connect with the alder tree's themes of air, emotion, and resilience, you might like to try this simple breathing exercise, which is designed to support the grounded release of feelings.

Close your eyes, bring your breathing into a steady rhythm, and call to mind a situation or feeling that you're currently finding difficult. Keep your breathing calm and consistent as you allow your thoughts to form and settle.

When you're ready, inhale slowly for a count of four, while focusing on the aspects of the feeling or situation that you'd like to move through or let go.

Hold your breath at the top of your inhale for two counts, really homing in on your emotions, then gradually exhale for a count of six, allowing your feelings to flow. Repeat this process for as long as you feel it is needed.

Self and Sound

Inspired by the alder's emphasis on music and self-expression, make a playlist that captures who you are and what you want to say at this point in time. What songs or sounds reflect your inner voice or sense of self right now?

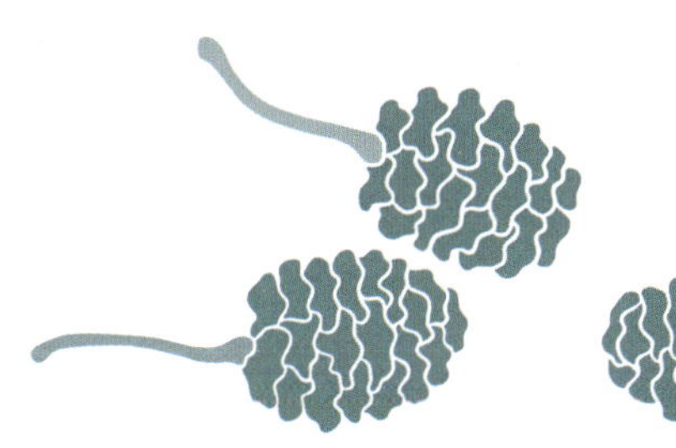

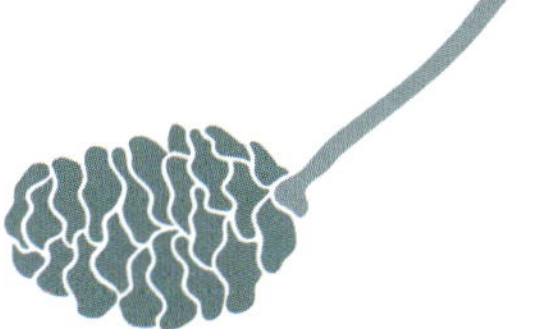

THE SAP MOON

Following February's cautious Snow moon comes the bolder Sap moon of March. This mid-spring lunar cycle reflects movement in the forests and woodlands. After lying dormant in the winter, shedding their leaves, and directing their sugar supplies down into their roots, deciduous trees begin to respond to the waxing days of spring. Sugar water rises again from their roots in the form of sap, and this sustenance is then channelled back up through the trunk towards the branches and twigs, ready to support the growth of new leaves.

The stirring of life beneath the surface that began in early spring continues, calling on us to likewise summon our energy and consider what it means to move up and outward, to reconnect with the wider world after the introspection of winter. Yet this rising energy is not without purpose: there is a tangible sense of direction, and reserves are distributed where they are most needed. This focus invites us to take action with intention and alignment, and to pay close attention to our own energy levels, for as the season takes hold there is a very real temptation to extend beyond our edges. Of course, come summer, this can often result in the wilting and exhaustion that comes with burnout, so it's essential to remember to rest and pause when needed, continuing to hold the theme of balance found in the symbolism of the Spring Equinox and the alder tree.

Rising Energy

Go outside and stand barefoot on the ground (on the bare earth or grass is best). Bend over and reach for your toes, so your body is curved and your head hangs low. Then, very slowly, begin to rise up, keeping your head down until you eventually return to standing upright again. As you rise, imagine a glowing, golden light rising through your body, energising every bone, every muscle, every organ. Continue this flow of light and energy by stretching your hands up to the sky and reaching up as high as you can.

Seeking Wisdom from the Sap Moon

What is rising in you?

✦

Where do you feel called to direct your energy right now?

✦

In what ways can you replenish your energy?

✦

Are there any areas of your life that are consuming too much energy?

✦

How might you make continued space for rest?

✦

In what ways might finding more balance help you in this season?

THE WAYFARER

Having welcomed our inner Maiden back in February in the form of the Initiate, in March we continue to connect with this childlike part of the self with the help of the Wayfarer. As the next evolution of the Maiden, the Wayfarer represents a sense of building curiosity and confidence, and a desire to step sure-footedly onto the path and see the world.

A voyager and adventurer, the Wayfarer sees the cycle of the year as a quest or pilgrimage: a purposeful journey towards a meaningful destination. Spring's emergence brings new horizons, and a desire for a map and markers to follow in order to explore life to its fullest. This intrepid outlook encourages us to turn vague ideas into more solid plans, getting clear on where we're heading and why it feels important. A wayfaring perspective also helps us to consider what we're seeking to gain from the voyage, what challenges we're likely to face along the way, and what supplies we need to stay on track.

This is not to say, however, that the Wayfarer always has to have a route mapped out. This part of ourselves is playful as well as practical and knows there is much to be gained from roaming free. Understanding that not all those who wander are lost, and that sometimes it's necessary to follow your heart as much as your head, the Wayfarer's internal compass also supports us in pursuing any new opportunities and experiences that may arise, without worrying too much about where they might lead us. This part of self knows that it's often the detours in life that offer the most unexpectedly beautiful views.

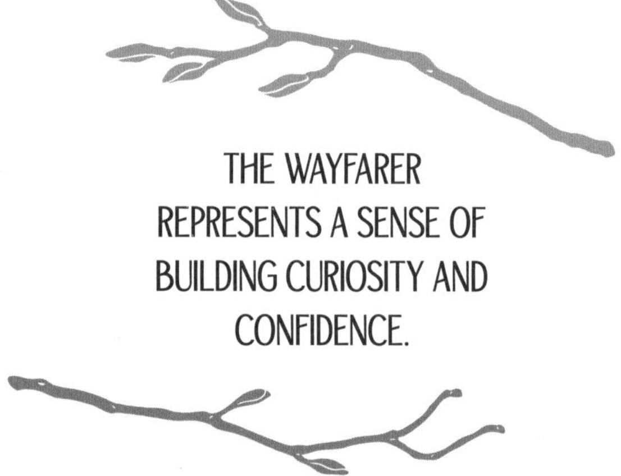

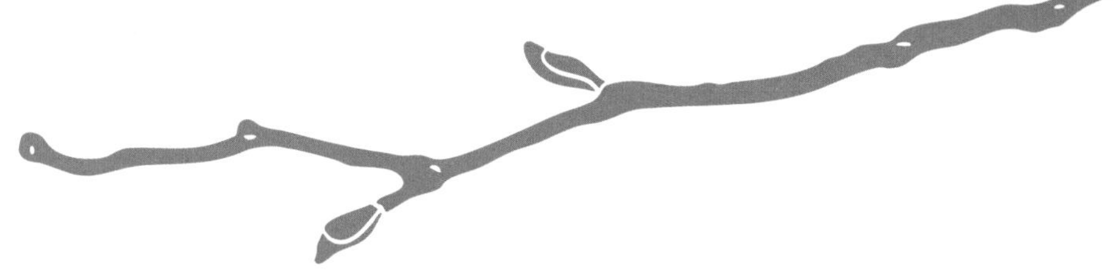

Mapping Your Journey

Guided by the theme of exploration, draw a map for the season or year ahead. Interpret the 'map' however you like – as a path, for example, or a circle divided into sections – then plot an overall destination (goal or vision) if you have one, plus any key 'landmarks' (events, deadlines) that you know you will encounter along the way.

Consider how you want to feel and what you might need as you 'make' this journey, and imagine the kinds of 'terrain' you might pass through along the way. Where might the hilly or boggy phases fall? Which stages are likely to offer easier walking?

YOUR SACRED SPACE

What could you add to your sacred space to represent the curious and adventurous Wayfarer? Suggestions include a map, a compass, or a picture of mountains or the rising sun.

THE HARE

Have you ever wondered where the phrase 'mad as a March hare' comes from? Look to the fields at this time of year and you might catch a glimpse of the boisterous boxing displays that have shaped the hare's frenzied reputation. Often wrongly assumed to be two males fighting over a female, the most vigorous boxers in fact tend to be the females themselves – either testing a male's strength and virility or fending off their overzealous pursuits. This behaviour is a sign of challenge or frustration, but its lively nature means it has come to be viewed as a symbol of the energy and vitality of spring, a season whose very name is associated with 'bounce'.

Despite this seasonal flurry of daylight activity, hares are primarily nocturnal creatures and generally shy and elusive. Mythologically, they're connected with the moon – particularly the full moon – and are honoured in many cultures as a representation of lunar energy. Eostre, a figure of Germanic origin honoured at the Spring Equinox (celebrated by some as Ostara, a pagan precursor to Easter), was said to transform into a hare at the full moon, perhaps laying the foundations for the modern Easter bunny. As a goddess of dawn and fertility, Eostre embodies spring's key theme of rebirth – not only in the literal context of welcoming new life, but also in the wider sense of embracing renewed energy, creativity, and possibility.

Move Like a Hare

Next time you're feeling in need of an energy boost, put on some music that makes you want to move your body and spend a few minutes dancing as spiritedly as a boxing hare. Even (or especially) if you feel self-conscious or worry you don't have time, try to embrace this opportunity to connect with the playful Air element and the vitality of spring, shaking off any lingering stagnancy. Afterwards, notice how you feel. Is there any difference in your mind and body?

SUNRISE

If we think of the year as a clock, March is equivalent to 6am. As such, at this time we welcome the dawn of the year, with many considering the Spring Equinox the 'true beginning' of the annual cycle. Astrologically the year starts with Aries season, which also begins at the Equinox, and there is a sense of rising energy, increased clarity, and illumination.

Dawn is a crepuscular time, when sunlight is present but has yet to reach its full potential, an 'on the cusp' moment and invitation to pause in liminality before entering the day fully. There are parallels here with the Equinox too, as we hold both the lunar energy of the night with the solar energy of the incoming day. The wisdom of the night was valued to such an extent by the ancient Celts that the day was said to begin at sunset rather than sunrise, which is reflected in the annual cycle that began with winter. So, while the symbol of the sunrise is indeed an opportunity to begin again, it carries with it echoes of the night and the wisdom we unearthed back in winter.

Greeting the Light

Try doing the Sap moon exercise as the sun rises, facing the east as you do so. You might also add a sun salutation stretch or choose to say the following words aloud:

I welcome you, light of the sun, and honour your energy, vitality, and life force.

Watch over me, empower me, as I step into this day.

APRIL

GROW

As April arrives, the rising energy that was palpable in early spring expands even further. In the wild world, we start to see the impact of this, with increasing temperatures, early morning birdsong, and gardens coming into bloom; in every respect, this phase of the year is connected to movement and prosperity. Aligning with this energy, we welcome the guiding word **grow**, but it's essential to question what growth means for you, as societal definitions typically focus on 'bigger and better', with the kind of growth that encourages richness and depth often forgotten. As energy levels increase, we may also feel called to take more focused action, to connect more with kith and kin, and to further develop our sense of self. It's time to integrate what has been explored and discovered over the winter months, to make that a tangible and real part of who we are.

THE ASH TREE

The ash tree is deeply connected to world mythology. In Norse legend, for instance, the ash (*Fraxinus*) was known as Yggdrasil, or the tree of life, which linked the nine lands and connected mortal men with the gods. Its centrality to a multitude of mythological stories has resulted in the ash being known by many as the World Tree, whose roots sink deep into the earth and feel the joy and pain of all living things. The ash's position at the centre of all life encourages us to deepen our understanding of our place in the world, and to acknowledge our deeply woven connection with all life on this planet.

As many ash trees are fading away due to ash dieback – a fungal infection that has spread across many parts of the world – this interconnection feels particularly poignant, and the ash's steady decline can be regarded as a metaphor for the wider plight of the natural world. But in response to the grief this may evoke, the ash reminds us to practise compassion and to think beyond our own immediate circles in order to support others – both human and more-than-human – with love and kindness.

Despite now declining in number, the ash tree was at one time connected to healing and purity, grown frequently beside holy wells in Ireland and springs on the Isle of Man. As a tree now in great need of these healing powers, the ash calls us to look to our own strong roots for guidance and support, so that we can hold steady during times of change, loss, and growth.

Honouring Interconnection

Draw three concentric circles. The inner circle represents you, and you might like to write your name in here. The next slightly larger circle represents your human kin – note down as many as you like, including friends, family, colleagues, acquaintances. Finally, the third and largest circle represents your more-than-human kin – again, note down as many as you like, including trees, landscapes, animals, and flowers, and try to be specific here with species or individuals.

Now spend a few minutes journalling in response to the following question:

How am I interconnected with my human and wild kin?

Caring for the Earth

How might you take care of your local landscape? This month, take one action that gives back to the trees in your area. You might like to plant a tree or give thanks to your local woodland – just do whatever feels possible and helps you to leave positive footprints.

THE SEED MOON

April is the month to plant seeds for the year ahead, both in the garden and in our lives and work. As the last full month of spring, it's a time when growth is rapid and colour begins to brighten our days once more; a welcome and invigorating change following the muted palette of the colder months. March's Sap moon welcomed the rising energy of the year, but with April's Seed moon we are invited to take action, commit, and plant our seeds for the months ahead. It is the final in a series of 'begin again' invitations that start with the rebirth of the sun at the Winter Solstice, before moving through the festivals of Imbolc and the Spring Equinox, and the new astrological year.

Here in late spring, we are offered one further opportunity to embrace this time of rapid growth and sow seeds for what it is we are reaching for. Solar energy is still rising and the earth has warmed, so it is fertile and ready for even more growth and new life. Come early summer, this rise will continue, but not with the same rapid speed of spring, and so we grasp for that which is growing within and commit to seeing through this cycle of beginnings.

Of course, not all planted seeds will grow, so while the Seed moon invokes action, creativity, and potential, it also requires trusting that the visions and plans meant for us will flourish with the burgeoning year.

Strengthening Intentions

Think of all the things that you want to accomplish this year, any changes you wish to make, or particular ways you want to feel. Now choose between one and three of these and follow the steps below for each.

Write down your intention.

Now ask yourself: *Why do I want this?* Respond intuitively for two minutes.

Then ask yourself: *What will change if this happens?* Respond for another two minutes.

And finally ask: *What is one step I can take today to move towards this intention?*

If you have access to seed paper, you may wish to use it for this exercise, so you can literally plant your intentions once they have been written.

Seeking Wisdom from the Seed Moon

How does it feel to 'begin again' with this lunar cycle?

✦

What do you want to recognise and seed in your life right now?

✦

What is growing in you?

✦

What still feels full of potential?

✦

What are you committed to nurturing and growing this year?

✦

Do your seeds have everything they need to grow?

THE WARRIOR

In April we embrace the third and final iteration of spring's Maiden archetype: the Warrior. How do you feel when you read that word? Does it further fuel the inner flame that you carefully tended with the goddess Brigid back in February, or does it make you want to retreat? For many of us, the idea of a warrior brings to mind battle language, words of force and aggression that can sometimes feel challenging and uncomfortable to explore.

Aligned with the solar part of self – the fire of action and purpose – there is nothing inherently 'wrong' with this interpretation of the Warrior as a fighter. In fact, although some people can be quick to anger and cause harm or damage, many others find 'fiery' emotions very difficult to process and express, choosing instead to suppress these feelings and suffer the resulting buildup of internal resentment, disconnection, or shame.

As such, it can often be profoundly transformative to learn to access our inner Warrior and advocate for ourselves when needed. There is an important and much overlooked distinction between fighting as a valid form of challenge or resistance and fighting as a violent attack.

Something that can help with this process is the concept of the *sacred* warrior: a heart-centred, passionate part of the self which is guided by values and vision. This version of the Warrior is tender but purposeful, stands strong in rooted beliefs, and is always ready to support, defend, and protect. A 'gentle activist' who is fierce yet kind, the Warrior in sacred form is committed to truth, justice, and the ripple effects that even small changes can bring when we all play our part. In late spring, our inner Warrior invites us to claim this part of our identity, and to use it for the good of self, others, and the wider world.

Embodying the Warrior

If you can, try a yoga flow incorporating a variety of warrior poses – either based on your own experience if you're familiar with these movements, or by searching online for a sequence you can follow. As you practise, channel the energy of the Warrior archetype in your mind and body: stand firm, move with purpose, and tune into a sense of heartfelt love for yourself and the world.

YOUR SACRED SPACE

What could you add to your sacred space to represent the passionate conviction of the Warrior? Suggestions include a small piece of rock, a symbol or drawing of a heart, or an affirmation of inner strength.

THE WARRIOR STANDS STRONG IN ROOTED BELIEFS AND IS ALWAYS READY TO SUPPORT, DEFEND, AND PROTECT.

THE WILD HORSE

A reflection of the Warrior archetype, the wild horse represents freedom, vigour, stamina, and strength – not only of body, but also of mind. When we see horses racing across heather-clad moors and open pastures, hooves thundering and tails and manes whipped by the wind, we imagine them to be high-spirited and strong-willed; self-assured and maybe a little stubborn.

Whether at rest or in motion, we recognise that these beings are different to their domesticated counterparts: although they are undoubtedly just as gentle at heart, they are wary and skittish, having no desire to be touched or tamed. When you catch their eye, they hold their ground, head held high and hooves planted firmly on the earth, but any sudden movements or hint of threat and they will proudly exercise their right to stamp or bolt.

As the final full month of spring, April teaches us to know and trust ourselves, so we will have the courage and confidence to advocate for what we need through the approaching season of summer. Whenever we are feeling unsure or overwhelmed, it can be helpful to call in the wisdom of the wild horse, to help us stand tall and run free.

Cultivating Inner Power

Think of a situation you're currently facing that calls for courage and confidence. When you have a clear example in mind, begin stamping your feet and clapping your hands vigorously, noticing the energy this generates and how it feels. As you continue, imagine yourself finding the courage and confidence to do what needs to be done or say what needs to be expressed. How could you channel this feeling of inner power to help you navigate your situation?

RAIN SHOWERS

The prospect of April showers may not seem particularly enticing, but there's plenty of wisdom to be found in this seasonal symbol! Rain is common at this time of year in the UK, alongside a general cooling or dampening that often occurs in between flashes of sunny spring days. This back-and-forth energy acts as a reminder for us to continue to seek out and create pockets of rest and slowness amid the rising solar energy.

Focusing on rain also invites us to connect with the Water element of autumn, counteracting the logical Air element of spring and encouraging us to regularly reflect and connect with our emotional self, which is symbolised by this fluid and changeable element.

While they may not always be welcome, rain showers can actually feel very refreshing at this time of year, as the freezing temperatures of winter have warmed and the rain is often light, dancing on pavements and pattering on roofs. It can also support us to shift the sluggish winter energy that often lingers into early and mid-spring. This revitalising quality allows rain to nourish our senses and, of course, reminds us that water in all its forms is essential for life.

Embrace the Rain

On the next rainy day, ditch the umbrella and head outside. Stand in the rain for a few moments or minutes, tipping back your head, closing your eyes, and feeling its transformative, cleansing impact on your skin. Make sure you smile, too!

SUMMER

FIRE | MIDDAY | MEADOW | MOTHER

Encapsulating the solar peak of the year, summer brings a feeling of vitality and abundance. Fuelled by the lively Fire element, the power of the midday sun, the restorative and richly diverse meadow soulscape, and the fierce but nurturing qualities of the Mother archetype, this season is a vibrant time of action and connection.

While this fullness can be deeply replenishing, it also poses challenges: the long, bright days and heightened activity can cause pressure or overstimulation, the heat can sometimes be draining, and it can be hard to balance daily responsibilities with the call of the wild and the longing to rest or roam. To stay grounded, it's important to make time for being alongside doing, through savouring slowness, nourishing the senses, and welcoming joy and pleasure in whatever ways feel needed.

MAY

IGNITE

The first of May, also known as May Day, brings the festival of Beltane and symbolises the gateway to summer. Long associated with vibrant community celebrations of fertility and abundance as the wild world comes into full bloom, this is a time of joy, play, creativity, and connection. As summer takes hold and we welcome the symbolic influence of the Fire element, we are encouraged to **ignite** our inner flame by pursuing the things that spark our passion for life. The weeks between Beltane and the Summer Solstice in June are fuelled by the highest solar energy of the yearly cycle, making May an ideal month for embracing the activities, ideas, people, and places that light us up.

THE HAWTHORN TREE

The hawthorn (*Crataegus*) – also known as the May Tree – is a potent symbol of power, pleasure, and life force. Its white blossom and the traditional image of the maiden-like May Queen adorned with a hawthorn crown evoke connections to fertility and lunar energy, yet its connotations of fruitfulness relate more closely to virility, dominance, and solar energy. As we welcome the season of summer, when solar energy reaches its peak, the hawthorn reminds us that we hold both energies within us.

Hawthorn bears the genus name *Crataegus*, which stems from the Greek word *kratos*, meaning 'strength'. In ancient Greek mythology, Kratos is strength personified in divine form. Unsurprisingly, therefore, the hawthorn is also connected with the dynamic and forceful element of Fire that comes to life in the summer, alongside its associations with passion and sensuousness.

The hawthorn's spiny thorns have earned it the reputation as a tree of protection – a quality also linked to its role as the Fairy Tree, guardian of the magical realm. Widely regarded as one of the most powerfully enchanted trees, it should be treated with the utmost reverence: some say that if you sit under a hawthorn tree on May Day, you could be whisked away to the spirit world never to return!

Sensing Pleasure

What sensory experience could you create to remind you to centre pleasure in your life? Respond to the prompts below to create your own pleasure ritual:

What brings you pleasure? How might you bring this into the ritual?

- **Scent ideas:** Essential oils, a candle, tea, herbs, or flowers
- **Taste ideas:** Fruit-infused water, your favourite meal or snack
- **Touch ideas:** Smooth or textured fabrics, tree bark, a smooth pebble, a soft feather
- **Colour ideas:** Clothing, decorative items, food (especially salads)
- **Sound ideas:** Running water, birdsong, a playlist or audio book, singing or playing an instrument

Establish Boundaries

One of the primary practical uses of hawthorn is for hedging, used to create boundaries between open spaces. As we welcome the most energetic phase of the year, what boundaries (physical, mental, emotional) do you wish to create in order to protect your own time and energy? List as many as you feel you need and consider how you can find the inner strength to uphold them.

THE HAWTHORN IS A POTENT SYMBOL OF POWER, PLEASURE, AND LIFE FORCE.

THE FLOWER MOON

The Flower moon welcomes the first flush of summer and celebrates the vitality and abundance of May. At this time, trees and hedgerows are adorned with blossom in all shades of pink and white, with hawthorn the crowning glory. This sense of blooming and flourishing encourages us to embrace the fullest expression of ourselves by connecting with others, trying out new things, making space for creativity, and seeking moments of delight.

Thinking back to the Sap and Seed moons of spring, we are encouraged in this first lunar cycle of summer to see the unfurling blossom as a symbol of the growth that has come from those previous months. Trusting that many of the flowers we see at this time of year will ultimately transform into juicy apples, pears, cherries, or plums as the seasons progress, May blossom also offers a heartening prophecy of the 'fruits' that are yet to ripen in our lives.

In meadows and gardens, many other plants also flower in early summer, following the dainty petals and pastel colours of spring with an explosion of bigger and brighter blooms, and reminding us of summer's call to embrace play and fun. Flowers – whether in the form of bouquets, wreaths, or crowns – have always played an important role in bringing beauty to celebrations and ceremonies, particularly when they are incorporated through the lens of floriography, the 'language' that reveals their hidden meanings. Connecting with this floral wisdom, whether decoratively or symbolically, is a lovely way to honour this vibrant part of the year.

The Gift of Flowers

One Beltane custom is the making and gifting of 'May posies': small bunches of flowers displayed in jam jars or similar. Usually tied with string hanging loops, these little floral tributes were traditionally left on the handles of front doors as a surprise offering of love and thanks for friends or neighbours.

Try making your own using cuttings from your garden if you have one, or a handful of responsibly foraged, non-protected wildflowers (or sprigs of blossom) mixed with foliage or herbs. For an extra layer of meaning, identify the feelings you want to convey and see if you can find flowers that symbolise your chosen sentiments – you'll find plenty of guidance online.

Arrange your posy in a jar or wrap it in paper or fabric, write an accompanying note if you like, and leave it on a loved one's doorstep to make them smile.

Seeking Wisdom from the Flower Moon

What makes you feel vibrant and alive?

✦

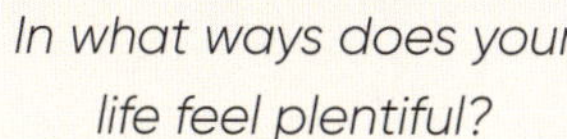

In what ways does your life feel plentiful?

✦

How could you help any areas that feel lacking to bloom?

✦

To what extent do you feel able to be your full self?

✦

How could you welcome more 'colour' (fun, play, boldness) into your days at this time?

✦

What hidden meanings or feelings do you long to express?

THE CREATRIX

As we ignite the flame of summer, the conviction and strength of April's Warrior archetype evolves to fuel the passionate and playful energy of the Creatrix, our guide for May. This part of self is the first facet of summer's overall Mother archetype and offers an alternative interpretation of 'mothering' that emphasises the value of producing and nurturing in their broadest sense, rather than being a specific reference to parenthood.

For many people and many reasons, the term 'mother' can feel heavy and complex, so the Creatrix offers a more neutral approach to exploring and embodying the concept of generative abundance. This perspective is inspired by Gaia or 'Mother Earth', the mythological figure who brings forth life of all kinds and reimagines 'fertility' as the gift of creativity. The word 'create' itself has etymological links to Ceres, the Roman goddess of agriculture, whose Greek counterpart is Demeter: a name thought by some to mean 'earth mother'.

THE CREATRIX CONNECTS US WITH OUR SPIRIT: OUR UNIQUE ESSENCE AND SOURCE OF VITALITY AND INSPIRATION.

The Creatrix connects us with our spirit: our unique essence and source of vitality and inspiration. As a version of the Mother archetype, this part of our psyche supports us to cultivate a strong sense of self, and to channel that into growth, connection, and the 'birth' of new ideas. Our inner Creatrix also helps us communicate our identity to the world and express the truth at our core, not only through typically creative outlets such as painting or poetry, but also through the way we think and innovate, and the way we present ourselves to the world – from the things we say and do to the music we listen to or the clothes we wear. The Creatrix knows that every choice is a reflection of who we are, and that life is a constant journey of self-creation and re-creation.

Meeting Your Creatrix

Make a creative representation of your inner Creatrix. For example, you could draw an intuitive self-portrait, compile a mood board, put together a playlist of songs, or write a letter from this part of yourself as a reminder of who you are.

YOUR SACRED SPACE

What could you add to your sacred space to represent the expressive spirit of the Creatrix? Suggestions include a paintbrush (or artistic tool of choice), a sprig of blossom or colourful flower, or a candle to represent your inner spark.

THE DRAGONFLY

Symbolising the spark of May, the dragonfly fittingly takes half its name from a mythical, fire-breathing creature. One of earth's oldest insect species, believed to have predated the dinosaurs, dragonflies are so named not only for their ancient origins, but also due to an alleged distortion of their Romanian folk name *calul-dracului*. In Romanian *drac* means 'devil', with the full term meaning 'devil's horse', but this is said to have been misinterpreted as 'dragon' when passing into English. In Chinese and some Indigenous North American traditions, dragonflies are thought to represent the souls of dragons.

Reflecting the solar qualities of summer, dragonflies are often associated with power and illumination. The word 'dragon' itself has etymological connections to themes of light, visibility, and seeing clearly, and in many cultures dragonflies are respected as wisdom-keepers and ancestral messengers, capable of revealing profound clarity and insight. Associated with Freya, Norse goddess of love and fertility, they are also symbols of the care, passion, and potential represented by the Fire element. This idea is further emphasised by the fact that pairs of dragonflies form a heart shape with their bodies when mating.

Perhaps most importantly of all, though, these fascinating insects offer a joyful reminder of our innate creativity, as is seen in their connection with the Mayan creativity goddess, Ix Chel. On a surface level, their jewel-like colours and intricate, stained-glass wings offer vibrant glimmers of colour and beauty, while their flitting flight patterns mirror the frenzied excitement that can come from being immersed in many plans and projects. The darting movements of dragonflies and the shape of their bodies have earned them a connection with sewing, while their ability to fly in any direction – including backwards – makes them a symbol of ingenuity and potential. Like the Creatrix, the dragonfly encourages us to believe that anything is possible.

Igniting Your Creativity

Write a list of all the ways you honour your creativity. Inspired by the dragonfly, try to think outside the box. Alongside any traditionally creative hobbies, consider things like cooking, interior design, bedtime stories, problem solving, idea generation, play, or anything else that uses your vision and imagination. If you're someone who has been told or believes that you're 'not creative', the results may be surprising! If you struggle to think of many (or any) examples, spend time contemplating how you could bring more creative energy into your life.

BLOSSOM

Deeply connected to the symbolism of the Flower moon cycle, blossom evokes themes of beauty, joy, pleasure, and abundance. Blooming throughout May, the blossom of the hawthorn tree in particular is present in British folklore. Long associated with fertility (see 'The Hawthorn Tree' earlier in this chapter), it is said that at Beltane, picking a sprig of hawthorn blossom and holding it close would help women attract a husband. Additionally, at Beltane both men and women would wash their hands and faces in the morning dew of hawthorn blossoms, a practice said to maintain or restore youth and bring prosperity of all kinds.

Alongside these hopeful associations, however, blossom is often connected with fragility, vulnerability, and the impermanence of life. Adorning trees only for a short time before drifting away on the wind, blossom has a beauty that is emphasised by its ephemerality – encouraging us to seek out joy in every moment – but it can also feel all too fleeting, offering a poignant reminder of life's inevitable changes and the ever-turning cycle of the seasons.

Inviting Abundance

Follow in the footsteps of those who have gone before you, and bathe in the morning dew of a blossom tree. Head out early, just after sunrise if possible, and find a hedgerow or easily accessible tree in full bloom. Greet the tree and ask for permission to receive its dew, before gently shaking its boughs (being careful to avoid any thorns!) to release the droplets onto your hands – perhaps splashing a little of the water on your face, too. As you do this, imagine the dew bringing you whatever feels like abundance right now.

JUNE

FLOURISH

June marks the midpoint and peak of the annual solar cycle. At the Summer Solstice, we are invited to step through the doorway into the waning half of the year – but until then, the wild world continues to thrive. Trees are in full leaf, gardens and vegetable patches are bountiful, colourful flowers are blooming, and the land has returned to green; this is a time to relish and enjoy the long, light days and the abundance of the earth. Here, at the pinnacle of the year, we are guided to consider what it means to **flourish**, without tipping into hyperstimulation or overwhelm, as can so often happen during high-energy phases. Above all, June invites us to celebrate the fullness of life, before the summer season gently begins to soften and slow.

THE OAK TREE

The oak tree builds on the characteristics of the hawthorn to offer perhaps the fullest expression of strength and power in the natural world. By June the mighty oak (*Quercus*) is in full leaf, resuming its crown as King of the Trees and mirroring the intense solar energy of midsummer. Rooted firmly in the ground but rising proudly to the sky, it is a tree synonymous with steadfastness, vigour, and endurance.

Oak trees are also associated with knowledge, experience, and longevity, due to the exceptionally long lives they can lead when left to grow naturally. They can live for up to 1,000 years, though 600 is a more common average, and it takes around 40 years of growth before they begin to yield acorns, with production peaking at the age of around 80 to 120 years. This timeline reveals the wisdom of a slow and sustainable approach, as well as the importance of staying rooted amid the intensity of midsummer. Furthermore, we might even lean into 'wintery' ways of being to support our health at this high point of the year, seeking slowness, valuing self-care, and honouring the capacity of our bodies.

THE OAK TREE OFFERS THE FULLEST EXPRESSION OF STRENGTH AND POWER IN THE NATURAL WORLD.

Finally, as we introduced in the December chapter, the oak tree is symbolically connected to the idea of doorways and thresholds. At the Summer Solstice it represents the 'doorway' to the waning half of the year, as the sun reaches its zenith and the gradual shortening of daylight hours begins once more. Mirroring the invitation of the Winter Solstice, we are once again asked to shed anything that no longer serves us, and to walk through midsummer's doorway with a sense of purpose that is rooted and alive.

Crossing the Threshold

Imagine that in front of you is a huge oak tree, with a door cut into its trunk. The door will lead you into the waning half of the year, but will only yield when you are ready, and to be ready, you must let go of everything that you no longer wish to be or believe, everything that you have carried with you over the past six months since the Winter Solstice (or perhaps for years or decades before that).

Consider now: *What must you lay down, in order to take your next steps?*

Remembering Your Strength

The oak tree reminds us to cultivate inner strength, but we often forget all the ways in which we are already strong. Write down – either on paper or on oak leaves you have collected – all the ways you have shown strength over the past six months. Place them on your desk or in your sacred space, or in a jar, and return to read them whenever it feels needed.

THE MEAD MOON

Honey is abundant throughout the month of June and was traditionally used prolifically during this period to make mead, the oldest known alcoholic drink. Its origins coincide with the introduction of beekeeping, raising the concept of the 'hive mind' of bees, and is a reminder of the importance of working hard together as a collective in order to achieve a goal.

Mead has been enjoyed at celebrations for millennia all across the world and is fairly simple to make, needing only honey, water, and yeast. Of course, to turn the concoction into an alcoholic drink requires fermentation, and it is no surprise that for many mythologies around the world, mead was seen as a magical potion, able to give anyone who drank it a potent combination of wisdom and inspiration. Further connections to creativity emerge from this symbolism, a reminder of the generative nature of this time of year and an encouragement for us to likewise connect with our own creative energies.

Alongside its links to magic and creativity, mead is often connected to themes of love and fertility. Mead was often consumed at celebrations such as handfasting (wedding) ceremonies, many of which took place in the month of June, and the happy couple were encouraged to drink generous amounts of it both on and after their wedding day to increase their chances of starting a family quickly. It's even thought that the term 'honeymoon' originates from this custom! These themes are reflected in the celebrated vibrancy of midsummer, with its invitation to rejoice in the warmth and light of the sun.

Healing Potential

In ancient mythology, mead was often referred to as 'the drink of the gods' and was allegedly given to warriors after a fight to enhance healing of their battle injuries. When you're feeling injured, hurt, or fearful, what has the potential or power to heal you? Write down a list of everything that comes to mind.

Seeking Wisdom from the Mead Moon

What feels sweet and abundant in your life right now?

✦

In what ways might you embrace a 'hive mind' mentality this month?

✦

What is currently in need of transformative magic?

✦

What do you feel called to create at this time?

✦

What does it feel like when you're in creative flow?

✦

What might you choose to celebrate at this peak of the solar year (especially small things)?

THE SOVEREIGN

As the sun reaches the peak of its summer fullness, we welcome the second and most luminous expression of the Mother archetype, the Sovereign. This part of our identity is our guiding light: a fearless leader, keeper of our courage, and source of our self-esteem. Associated, as with all things summer, with solar energy and fire, the Sovereign continues the work of the Creatrix – fuelling our passions, sparking our inspiration, and breathing life and love into our spirit to support a heart-centred way of being. Much like the Warrior of late spring, the Sovereign's presence is one of fierce tenderness; a nourishing warmth paired with keen-eyed insight and strong-willed belief. When this part of self is burning brightly, we can move forward with clarity and integrity.

As can be seen from the traditional interpretation of the sun sign in astrology as our primary persona, the sun is strongly associated with ego and the self. The Sovereign has a similar focus, encouraging us to explore and pursue wholeness, authenticity, autonomy, and individuality. Alongside independence, though, this archetype also prioritises *inter*dependence: the idea of being both singularly complete and part of a wider community. Although the Sovereign honours the self, it is never at the expense of others, for true sovereignty recognises that 'oneness' requires integration rather than separation.

This interconnectedness extends to the Sovereign's relationship with power, which, as a version of a Queen or Empress archetype, is welcomed – but in a non-hierarchical way. Rather than seeking to overpower, the Sovereign seeks to *em*power: to *give* strength and potential rather than take it away. Although the word 'sovereign' makes reference to the act of reigning, the related Latin word *regerer* means not only 'to rule' but also 'to keep straight'. More like a ruler in the sense of the measuring tool than a monarch, the Sovereign therefore acts as a guide; a source of direction and alignment, both for the self and others.

WHEN THIS PART OF SELF IS BURNING BRIGHTLY, WE CAN MOVE FORWARD WITH CLARITY AND INTEGRITY.

The Light in Your Life

Draw a large circle, and inside it write down all the things you value about yourself.

Around the outside of the circle, draw lines (as many as you need) to represent both the rays of the sun and the people or beings in your life who you love, and who love and support you in return.

Display this 'sovereign sun' as a symbol of your inner light and the light of your community.

If you want to keep this power with you more closely, find or make a sun- or fire-themed pendant to wear as a daily reminder of your Sovereign self.

YOUR SACRED SPACE

What could you add to your sacred space to represent the empowering flame of the Sovereign? Suggestions include a coin as a reflection of worth, a photograph that captures the 'real you', a jar of honey, or a bee or sun symbol.

THE QUEEN BEE

Associated with both leadership and community, the queen bee is a perfect symbol of the Sovereign self. Influencing the efforts of the colony's worker bees (fellow females) by releasing powerful pheromones, the queen bee may seem controlling, but her power is only exerted for the greater good of the hive. The queen alone has the capacity to reproduce, and there can only be one queen at a time, meaning she is solely responsible for the future of the colony.

The primary focus of the queen bee is laying eggs. She produces thousands of eggs each day, and in return she is cared for like royalty by the workers, who manage the daily running of the hive. It is a small-scale example of self in service to society, which mirrors the 'village' of motherhood: the interconnected system of reciprocal support it can take to raise the next generation.

The queen's continual reproductive cycle reflects the way that summer sun can draw us towards relentless action, and reminds us of the need to balance productivity with rest and self-care to avoid burnout. Here it can be helpful to look to June's Mead moon for support: as a drink made from honey, the product of the bees' hard work, it encourages us to savour the sweetness of life amid the busy hum of doing and achieving. When focus and high energy take hold, this can be something our inner Sovereign needs help to remember.

Savouring Sweetness

The queen bee inspires us to make space for pleasure alongside productivity. Is this something that you do in your own life? Take a few moments to think of a few things you desire, but that perhaps feel 'too indulgent' to actively pursue. Now consider how you could allow yourself to sink into the sweetness of one or two of these things, or at the very least bring some aspect of them into your days in a small and achievable way. Is there a summer ritual you could create based on your ideas?

THE WILD ROSE

Like many species of rose, the wild rose is symbolic of love, affection, and adoration. Beautiful to observe, it also has a heady scent, connected to pleasure and sensuality. In June, roses offer their most vibrant displays and are full of life, attracting bees, moths, and a whole host of other insects. They remind us to grasp our own life-force energy, to notice what makes us feel most alive, and to embrace it fully.

Wild roses are often known to ramble across hedges, fences, and buildings, seeking out the sunniest, warmest spots and lingering in these places. We may follow suit in our own lives at this time of year, following our hearts, being curious and open to adventure, and making sure we savour whatever life has to offer.

Rose-Infused Energy

Head outside and gather some rose petals. Steep the petals in some water, or for a quicker result, bring to the boil in a saucepan and simmer for around 10 minutes or until the pigment has been released from the petals.

Strain and remove the petals, allow the water to cool (if need be), and then pour into a spray bottle with a splash of alcohol (vodka is ideal) to preserve if you wish.

Use the rose-infused water as a room spray to remind you of your own life-force energy whenever you need a boost.

JULY

NURTURE

July is the last month of high summer and, though the days remain long and light, by this point in the year the power of the sun is gradually beginning to wane and the Fire element becomes a slower, softer presence. There is still a sense of abundance all around, but nature's focus is no longer directed towards new growth: instead, there is an invitation to **nurture** that which has already come to fruition. In our daily lives, it can help to have a similar approach as we seek to balance productivity with rest or adventure, while navigating the challenges and distractions that sunny days and warm weather can bring. The call to tend to ourselves is a compassionate reminder to soak up the summer while we can, in whatever ways feel needed and nourishing.

THE HOLLY TREE

Although we might typically think of the holly (*Ilex*) as a winter tree, its placement here in late summer is particularly potent. As the reign of the Oak King comes to an end at the Summer Solstice, the Holly King takes the crown, and turning to this evergreen tree offers an essential reminder that although it might feel like growth and light are continuing as before, there has been a shift from expansion to contraction, no matter how imperceptible. Offering nourishment to navigate this transition, the holly represents the continuation of hope and vitality, and is associated with themes of immortality, energy, and protection.

This protection was believed to extend to the elements, with holly trees traditionally planted in gardens and close to houses to guard against evil spirits and lightning. Perhaps this stemmed from a mythological connection to thunder gods such as the Norse Thor and the Celtic Taranis, but the spines on holly leaves are also said to act as tiny lightning conductors, which would indeed protect not only the tree but also objects nearby.

As a plant with separate male and female specimens, holly also represents balance and encourages us to pay attention to the dualities of life: light and dark, plenty and scarcity, courage and fear, love and animosity. Holly gently invites us to use our inner wisdom to guide our outward action.

Protecting Your Lunar Self

Add a sprig of holly to your sacred space as a way of protecting your energy and boundaries, and to honour your lunar self at this solar time of year.

Inner and Outer Selves

Draw a vertical line on a piece of paper. On the left, write all the things your lunar/inner self currently needs or desires (for example, more sleep, time to yourself, clarity). Then, on the right, note down how your solar/outer self might take action to support this need or desire. For example, if your lunar self desires more time to yourself, your solar self might act by adapting your calendar plans for the next two weeks to create this space.

THE HAY MOON

As midsummer gives way to late summer, the fields turn from lush green to rippling gold with the approach of harvest season, and the haymaking that began in June continues into July. Summer is a season in which many aspects of life compete for our attention: adventure, rest, family responsibilities, and social plans all sit side by side with work, and we can feel scattered and distracted. But if we look to nature at this point in the year, her energy is no longer being directed into frenzied growth; instead her focus has shifted to maturing and ripening. Ideally, then, late summer is a time to step back from the continual quest for productivity in order to tend to other areas of life.

The Hay moon encourages us to 'make hay while the sun shines' – to embrace spontaneity, prioritise fun and well-being, and soak up the warmth and light while we can. It's important to note that this process will look different for everyone: some may lean into the high solar energy and enjoy filling the long, light summer days with activities, while others require a softer approach focused on savouring small pleasures.

As a counter to the societal narrative that pushes us to stay in the energy of high summer forever, this lunar cycle gives us much-needed permission to slow down, drawing our attention to the drying of the grass, the turning of the season, and the waning of the year.

Prioritise Fun

Inspired by the Hay moon's focus on fun and spontaneity, gather 10–20 small scraps of paper and fill them with all the light-hearted things you'd like to do this season – whether these are activities you enjoy every summer or ideas you've always wanted to try but have never got round to. (Make sure they're things that fit your current budget and energy levels.)

When you've finished, fold the scraps of paper in half and store them in an empty jar. Next time you have some free time, pull out one of your suggestions and go and have fun!

Seeking Wisdom from the Hay Moon

In what ways do you feel scattered, distracted, or pulled in different directions?

Where is your life slowing and in need of tending right now?

Does summer make you feel recharged or depleted, and why?

What pressures or expectations about summer could you let go of?

What would your version of an ideal summer look and feel like?

How could you 'make hay while the sun shines' this season?

THE GUARDIAN

July's arrival brings us the final face of the Mother archetype: the Guardian. With the sun's energy waning slightly now, this evolution reveals the lunar side of the solar self – the gentle warmth of a nurturing caregiver, who encourages rest and replenishment. In previous chapters we have touched on the way that love shows up as heart-centred passion in the summer, but here in the later weeks of the season, that burning fire softens and slows, transforming into love as devotion: a practice and a promise, directed both towards and beyond the self.

In individual terms this might look like honouring your needs, protecting and upholding boundaries, taking time to rest, or revisiting rituals and routines that may have drifted. More widely, it could mean offering support to others, cultivating community, or spending time in the wild world in a quiet way that allows space for deeply felt connection and gratitude.

When being guided by the outwardly directed giving part of the Guardian, it's important to keep back some of that love and devotion for ourselves, too. One key risk of the wider Mother archetype is the potential for martyrdom, resentment, and burnout due to prioritising care of others over care of self, so the Guardian – like the holly tree – reminds us to seek and maintain a healthy balance here, and to be open to receiving alongside giving.

THE GENTLE WARMTH OF A NURTURING CAREGIVER, WHO ENCOURAGES REST AND REPLENISHMENT.

Taking Care of Yourself

It's become a well-worn cliché to associate self-care with having a bath, but it remains a beautiful way to connect with your inner Guardian. In the summer, when the Fire element is burning fiercely, one way of 'cooling' that intensity and reducing overstimulation can be found in turning to the Water element for soothing refreshment. This is especially true in July, when we're already looking for ways to access the softer, lunar-leaning qualities of the season.

If you have access to a bathtub, make some time for a peaceful, replenishing soak – lighting candles, playing restful music, and adding any calming salts, oils, herbs, or flowers that you have available. For a deeper experience, plan your bath to coincide with the full Hay moon, so you can make the most of the high lunar energy to balance out the midsummer sun.

Those without a bath could try going for a swim, visiting a river or lake, immersing their face or feet in a bowl of chilled water, or drinking a night-time tea blend before bed.

YOUR SACRED SPACE

What could you add to your sacred space to represent the gentle, nurturing Guardian? Suggestions include soft fabric, a smooth pebble, or a picture or symbol of the moon.

THE VIXEN

While undeniably shining with solar qualities such as leadership, cunning, instinct, and resourcefulness, the Vixen also beautifully represents the lunar-influenced mother figure epitomised by the Guardian. As excellent diggers who seek safety underground, and crepuscular beings most active at dawn and dusk, foxes are comfortable with the shadowlands of life beneath the surface and at the edges of the day. This sense of feeling at home in the half-light is apt for July, the month when the holly takes over from the oak and the Hay moon hints at the drying and fading to come. The fox, and more specifically the Vixen, with her aptitude for provision and protection, reminds us of late summer's call to begin turning gradually inwards once again.

Foxes live in groups in which the primary family – a dog and a vixen, plus their cubs – is sometimes joined by other adult females who offer support to the dominant vixen. Cubs are born in the spring, and over the summer they build independence in preparation for leaving the den when autumn arrives. In late summer, therefore, vixens find themselves navigating the phase of motherhood between caretaking and letting go, just as the Guardian archetype holds the outer work of nurturing others alongside the inner work of nurturing self.

A Dusk Walk

Go for a walk at dusk to allow yourself to be enveloped by the fading of the day. Look out for foxes if they're common in your area, and open your senses to all that's present as the light dwindles: the scent of warm earth or floral fragrances drifting on the breeze; the fluttering of moth wings; the first glints of stars emerging in the sky; the calling of birds as they settle down for sleep. Notice what it feels like to occupy this space between day and night, and consider how you might balance solar and lunar energy within yourself.

THUNDERSTORMS

Low rumbles of thunder and burning flashes of lightning occur most frequently in a summer sky, offering release from the intensity of building pressure and heat. Storms are so common in North America at this time of year that July's full moon is known by some as the Thunder moon. The combination of sound and light present in a thunderstorm is one of the most elemental and powerful displays in nature, reminding us of the incredible life force that is present not only in the wild world, but also in ourselves.

Now the peak of midsummer has passed, plants and flowers can often appear to wilt under the continued intensity of the sun, which still wields a great deal of power throughout the month of July, but the transformative nature of rain storms will often freshen and re-green the landscape, at least for a short time. The water balances out the heat of the sun and brings a different kind of energy, one that can often feel like relief, giving permission for us to likewise find ways to counteract the busy action of this phase.

Lifting the Pressure

On some sticky notes, or on small pieces of paper, write yourself a series (maybe three to five) of permission slips, intended to ease the pressure we can often feel at this time of year. Begin with the phrase 'You have permission to...' each time and add your own endings, perhaps responding to anything you feel you *should* be doing at this time of year. For example:

You have permission to rest in the middle of the day, even if it feels like you don't have the time.

AUTUMN

WATER | DUSK | RIVER | MYSTIC

As summer fades away, we welcome the fourth and final season of the cycle. Autumn's arrival brings the cooling ripples and emotional depth of the Water element and the healing release of the river soulscape. Connected to dusk and the fading light, this is a season of softening and sinking; a time to invoke the intuitive magic of our inner Mystic.

In early autumn, the fields are golden and the hedgerows are fruitful. There is a flurry of activity as the harvest is gathered in, and we scurry to soak up the energy and light of the sun as it begins to wane more rapidly. By late autumn, the wild world is preparing for the colder months ahead and, once the leaves change colour and begin to fall, we too are encouraged to transform and let go, readying ourselves for the turning of the year as winter approaches once again.

AUGUST

SOFTEN

The arrival of the festival of Lammas as August begins signals the threshold between summer and autumn. As with all transitions, this can often seem like a liminal time with one foot in each season, feeling the flare of midday sunlight while also picking blackberries, spending warm evenings outdoors while also noticing an early morning chill. Through an agricultural lens, it can be helpful to think of August as a mini season in its own right – 'harvest season' – and we can expand this by reflecting on our own lives too, taking time to collect, sort through, and consider what we want to let go of and what we want to hold on to as we move further into autumn. Above all, this is a month to **soften**; to mellow, slow, and sink into the ripening richness of the harvest.

THE HAZEL TREE

With their hand-sized leaves and frilly-coated nuts, hazel trees (*Corylus*) bring a playful presence to hedgerows and woodlands at this time of year. Historically, hazel has been used for a wide range of purposes, including for fencing, divining rods, woven baskets, and as staffs or walking sticks. Their nuts provide essential sustenance for animals such as dormice as they prepare for hibernation, and this gathering of nourishment marks the shift of nature's attention towards the need to prepare for the colder months ahead. We can also consider what it means to gather our own 'soul food' – experiences and inspiration to see us through the darker days to come. That might look like simply soaking up the sun, exploring wild places, making memories with friends and family, or tending to our own well-being.

The hazel has long been revered in many cultures across the world, and in one ancient tale nine hazel trees were said to hang over a well or pool of knowledge. As their nuts fell into the water, 'wisdom bubbles' formed that then ran downstream, sometimes consumed by salmon, which, when eaten, were said to pass on these mystic powers. This connection to wisdom is unsurprising when you consider that hazelnuts contain within them everything they need to grow when the time is right. This month we may ask ourselves this question:

Can I tune into my own untapped wisdom, and trust in its presence and power?

HAZELNUTS CONTAIN WITHIN THEM EVERYTHING THEY NEED TO GROW WHEN THE TIME IS RIGHT.

Finding Your 'Soul Food'

What does 'soul food' look like for you? Write a list of all the ways you could nourish yourself with soul food in this harvest phase of the year, preparing for the darker days ahead.

Seeing Your Truth

Try an open-eye meditation to connect with your own inner wisdom. Look at yourself in a mirror and allow your gaze to soften. Hold the following question in your mind: *What do I know to be true?* Stay here and look in the mirror for as long as feels comfortable.

THE GRAIN MOON

After the Hay moon of July, we welcome the next phase of harvest season with August's Grain moon. This lunar cycle signals that now is the time to survey the 'fields' of our lives and gather our own 'crops' – in other words, to check in with our plans and projects and sort the wheat (good things to be celebrated) from the chaff (things that can be discarded).

This process is a key phase in the agricultural cycle and, although it is not widely celebrated today, its significance would have traditionally been signalled by the festival of Lammas on 1st August, the name of which derives from the Old English term *hlaf-mas*, meaning 'loaf mass'. At this time, loaves of bread were baked from the freshly gathered wheat, and corn dollies – small figures woven from the stalks of field crops – would have been made to honour the spirit or deity of the harvest.

Central to this time of year is the knowledge that each harvest holds not only the current year's abundance, but also the seed of all future harvests. We might turn here to stories of the Grain Mother for guidance, a full and fertile figure represented across different cultures. In ancient Greek mythology, for example, she is Demeter - said to personify the whole of the harvest - while her daughter Persephone represents the individual grains or seeds, signalling the potential for future new life that will lie dormant until the energy of the earth rises again in the spring.

This month we might think of our own collection of 'grains' or 'seeds' (our ideas and visions for the future), and what we wish to hold safe throughout the darker seasons until the energy of the world begins to increase once more.

Gathering Your Grains

Imagine your dreams and ideas for the future as grains. Choose five of these ideas and write them down on individual scraps of paper. You might choose to 'plant' them in the earth (if you use special seed paper), burn them (safely!) on a fire, or keep them in a journal or your sacred space – it doesn't matter which ritual you choose; just do something that feels meaningful to you.

Seeking Wisdom from the Grain Moon

If you were to survey the 'fields' of your life, how do they make you feel?

What is your metaphorical 'wheat'? (What do you have to celebrate?)

What is your metaphorical 'chaff'? (What do you wish to let go of?)

Who are you particularly grateful for right now?

Which more-than-human kin (trees, animals, and so on) are you also grateful for?

How might you express your gratitude for both human and more-than-human kin this month?

THE ALCHEMIST

In the liminal space between summer and autumn, we welcome a new archetypal energy shaped by the qualities of the Mystic. Ephemeral and changeable, just like the incoming season itself, this overarching character guides us on the descent into the darker months, lighting the way with magic. Against August's backdrop of golden fields and glowing light, the Alchemist is the first incarnation of the Mystic that we meet on this journey.

Historically, the mysterious art of alchemy is said to have been devoted to two lofty pursuits: finding a way to turn base metals into gold and seeking the elixir of eternal life. Over time, the term has come to be used more generally to describe any process involving transformation or amalgamation. Looking more deeply into its swirling cauldron of symbolic meanings, there are also glints of themes such as healing, dissolution, and reframing the ordinary as something precious.

Throughout August, we're guided by the Alchemist to apply these ideas to our lives. It's a month of transition, as we've already explored, and as summer gradually blends into autumn, many of us have a bubbling melting pot of work, holidays, social gatherings, and family responsibilities to attend to. The softening described at the start of this chapter can be experienced as a kind of disintegration, as areas of life overlap and boundaries blur. Routines and structures often slip at this time of year, and even our own sense of identity can begin to dissolve as we drift away from our familiar flow.

THE ALCHEMIST ENCOURAGES US TO LOOK FOR THE GOLDEN MOMENTS ALONG THE WAY.

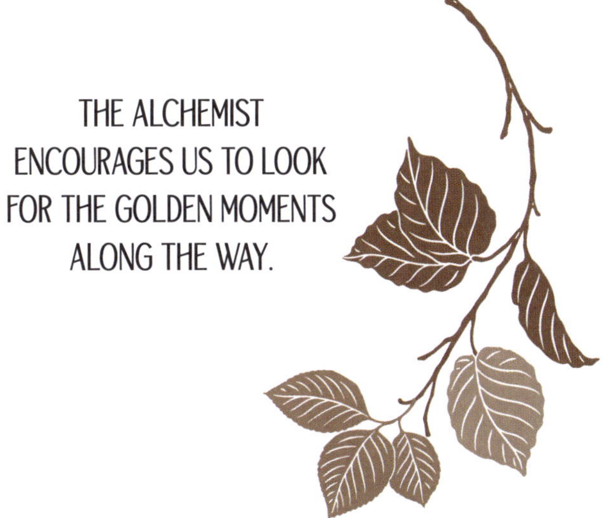

To navigate this phase, we're called upon to soften *ourselves:* to loosen our grip and allow the fluidity and trust that things will re-solidify on the other side of the transition. The Alchemist encourages us to put our faith in mystery, to make space in our lives for compassion, and to look for the golden moments along the way. 'Gilt over guilt' is this archetype's mantra!

Find Your Glimmers

In psychology, the opposite of triggers (things perceived as threats by our nervous system) are known as 'glimmers' – small, everyday moments of joy, beauty, or connection that help us feel calm and content. Guided by the Alchemist, consider your glimmers, so you can hold them close at difficult times.

YOUR SACRED SPACE

What could you add to your sacred space to represent the mellow merging of the Alchemist? Suggestions include something gold, a nut, or an ear of grain.

THE DORMOUSE

In Britain and Europe, the native species of dormouse – *Muscardinus avellanarius* – is known specifically as the hazel dormouse, after its primary food source. This tiny, reclusive creature is rarely seen, but is often portrayed curled up with its tail wrapped around its face and body for warmth. A comforting symbol of August's invitation to soften, dormice are synonymous with rest.

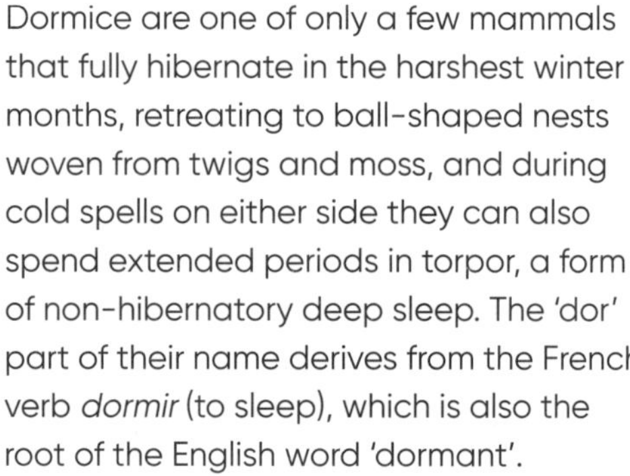

Dormice are one of only a few mammals that fully hibernate in the harshest winter months, retreating to ball-shaped nests woven from twigs and moss, and during cold spells on either side they can also spend extended periods in torpor, a form of non-hibernatory deep sleep. The 'dor' part of their name derives from the French verb *dormir* (to sleep), which is also the root of the English word 'dormant'.

With a coat the colour of golden harvest grain, the soft, sleepy dormouse offers a gentle symbol of August's pull to surrender, and also a timely reminder to seek nourishment and replenishment ahead of autumn's incoming flurry of energy.

Sinking into Rest

Inspired by the dormouse, try a yoga nidra practice – this is a kind of meditation that is experienced lying down and designed to induce a state of deep relaxation or 'conscious sleep'. You'll find lots of free videos to follow online, or you might like to attend a class nearby where your rest can be guided and supported in person.

GOLDEN FIELDS

Connected to the lunar cycles of July and August, this month's symbol refers to crops such as wheat and barley that often appear golden in the early autumn light. There is a sense that the fields appear as 'liquid gold' as they ripple in the wind, representing the 'riches' or abundance of the year. It's easy to imagine the hard work of harvesting stretching back across the centuries, and the feeling of satisfaction and also relief as the crops were gathered in and communities reaped what had been sown earlier in the year.

Today, the fields are a human-made monocultural presence in our landscape, but these spaces still provide a home for many wild beings in their more diverse edgelands – wildflower margins, stray poppies or cornflowers – symbolising the presence of wildness in all places. This invites a deeper consideration of the human–nature relationship, and the ways in which wildness and society or culture can coexist both in our individual lives and also on a wider collective scale.

Rewilding in the Margins

Note down all the ways you are already welcoming wildness into your life. Then consider: in what ways could you welcome wildness into the 'edgelands' of your days? Think of small moments to help you here – morning or evening rituals, mealtimes, and so on. You might choose to try these just for the month or during the season of autumn as a whole.

SEPTEMBER

GATHER

Building on the arrival of harvest season in August, September calls us to continue the process of surveying and collecting. As the month of the Autumn Equinox – the doorway to the heart of autumn – this is a time of ripeness, abundance, and gratitude. As in the spring, the Autumn Equinox offers a moment of solar balance before a period of dynamic change, but here the next phase involves sinking into darkness rather than rising towards the light. The focus, therefore, turns towards completion and preparation ahead of winter, and we are encouraged in many ways to **gather**. Whether by foraging in the woods, harvesting crops from the garden, coming together in community, bringing ideas to fruition, or seeking clarity on future plans, 'gathering' in all senses of the word can help us make ready for the darker months and the new cycle beyond.

THE BLACKTHORN TREE

In the Celtic tree calendar, the period from 2nd to 29th September was traditionally referred to as the month of *muin* (pronounced 'moo-in'), after the eleventh character of the Ogham alphabet ᚋ. *Muin* most commonly tends to be translated as 'vine', but some scholars suggest that its meaning may actually refer to a thorny thicket, like the blackthorn tree.

Sometimes known as the Dark Crone of the Woods, the blackthorn (*Prunus spinosa*) has a sinister reputation. Its branches are barbed with long and sharply pointed spines which, if embedded deeply into the skin, can cause painful inflammation of the nearest joints, and it is often superstitiously regarded as a harbinger of misfortune. At the same time, however, its bark, leaves, flowers, and fruit are also known for their cleansing properties, making it a tree highly valued by healers and herbalists.

As both a cause of illness and a remedy for restoring health, the blackthorn reminds us once again of the complex and interwoven dualities of life – a theme befitting the Autumn Equinox, with its focus on equilibrium. This sense of balance and opposition is also reflected in the life cycle of the tree itself, which produces delicate, white flowers in early spring, reflecting the returning light, and sour, blue-black sloes in autumn, signalling the descending darkness.

As an often misunderstood member of the wild world, the blackthorn teaches us not to take things at face value, but to look more deeply and welcome new perspectives. This invitation to explore beneath the surface also connects the blackthorn with intuition and the wisdom of the subconscious; an important reminder as autumn draws us back towards the shadows of our inner worlds.

THE BLACKTHORN REMINDS US OF THE COMPLEX AND INTERWOVEN DUALITIES OF LIFE.

Searching the Shadows

Although an autumn tree, the blackthorn's midnight-coloured berries and introspective qualities invite us to mentally make ready for the oncoming darkness of winter. Close your eyes and focus your attention on your breath, slowing and steadying. When we close our eyes it can often feel as though we are plunged into darkness, but stay a while and you will notice shapes and colours begin to appear. Look deeper, and notice how this shadowy, shapeshifting space makes you feel.

Sit with your eyes closed, looking with curiosity for as long as you feel able, and then when you are ready, spend a few minutes journalling in response to the following question:

What is waiting for you in the shadows?

Nourishment and Preparation

Sloes are rich in vitamins and antioxidants, and can be transformed into potent remedies to support seasonal wellbeing. How might you focus on healing and health throughout autumn and into winter? You could make fire cider, take a vitamin D supplement, or find ways to include gentle movement in each day. Choose three actions to take this month to nourish your body in preparation for the colder, darker months ahead.

THE BRAMBLE MOON

Once known as *dris-muine* (prickle thorn) in Scots Gaelic, the bramble represents another variety of the 'thorny thicket' that could be indicated by *muin*, the Ogham character of September. Since, as we've already explored, *muin* is more usually translated as 'vine', September is often associated with grapes, and the month's full moon is sometimes referred to as the Wine moon. We choose instead to think of this as the cycle of the Bramble moon, as blackberries (the fruit of the bramble) can also be used for wine-making and have long been gathered from the hedgerows at this time of year.

As an alcoholic drink, wine has the potential to impact perception, lower inhibitions, and cause fluctuations in mood, thereby linking the Bramble moon to self-expression, inner truth, passion, and wrath. Given the connection between intoxication and unpredictable behaviour, and the alchemical nature of the wine-making process, this lunar cycle can also be related to the key autumnal themes of change and transformation.

Like the blackthorn tree, the bramble is spiky in nature and its barbed tendrils symbolise strong emotion, as well as overcoming difficulty and growing through experience by learning from past pain or mistakes. At the same time, the deep colour, syrupy juice, and intense flavour of blackberries reflect the richness of life and the abundance of the harvest, reminding us to cherish our blessings alongside acknowledging our challenges.

Note: The closest moon to the Autumn Equinox, which usually falls in September, is also known as the Harvest moon.

Gathering Gratitude

Forage for some blackberries if you can. Choose a seasonal recipe – jam, a pie or crumble, cordial or wine – then seek out a local bramble patch and gather as many berries as you need, making sure to leave plenty for your wild neighbours. As you pick, reflect on the things you feel most grateful for at this time, then imagine the goodness of those gifts infusing into whatever you make.

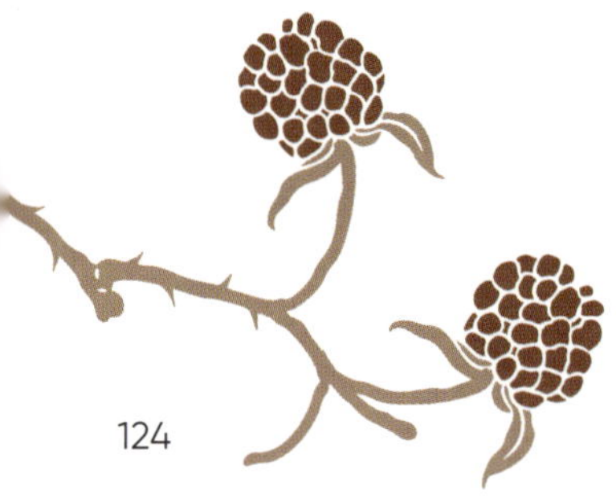

Seeking Wisdom from the Bramble Moon

In what ways are you 'prickly' (sharp, defensive, protective), and why?

What truths or emotions are you hiding that you would like to express more freely?

What feels changeable or unpredictable in yourself or your life right now?

How does the theme of richness feel relevant for you this season or this year?

What hurts or struggles have you experienced that have helped you grow?

What gifts or blessings can you gather and hold close to your heart at this time?

THE WEAVER

After the drifting and dissolving that we experience in August, the next facet of the Mystic archetype, the Weaver, arrives to help us find our way back to wholeness. In the context of our sense of self, the Weaver interprets September's focus on gathering as a pull towards reintegration and reconnection; an opportunity to draw together the disparate threads of our lives – untangling them where necessary – in order to re-entwine them in a simpler, more coherent pattern.

Often this process manifests as the common 'back to school' desire to revisit intentions and re-establish routines, as the rhythm of our societal calendar converges with the scurrying autumnal preparations of the wild world. (We'll return to this idea shortly with the help of this month's animal guide, the squirrel.) On a deeper level, though, this focusing of attention turns our awareness back towards our inner world after the outward-facing months of summer, prompting us to assess not only how and where we are, but *who* we are.

More than just a gatherer of threads, the Weaver is also a spinner of yarns. A gifted storyteller, this archetype helps us sift through the narratives we hold about ourselves and the world, and to rewrite them where necessary. Weaving words and drawing on a powerful interconnection with 'oneness' – the spirit or essence that flows through all of us – this part of the self blends reality with the mythic imagination, and unites the wisdom of past, present, and future to help us cocreate a new vision of our place within the web of life. Echoed in the whispers of tree roots and mycelial networks, the message of the Weaver guides us from messy entanglement to elegant enchantment.

Weaving Words

Write the story of your year so far, either in full if that feels right, or as a series of chapter headings representing each significant event or phase. Make sure to give your story a title that reflects its overall essence. When you've finished, try to distance yourself from the narrative a little, perhaps rereading it through the eyes of a friend. Then ask yourself:

* *Does the whole story still feel true?*

* *Which parts of the story (if any) would I like to rewrite?*

* *Who am I right now according to this story?*

* *What story do I want to write for the rest of the year?*

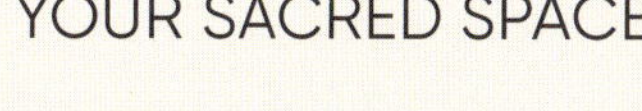

YOUR SACRED SPACE

What could you add to your sacred space to represent the interlacing threads of the Weaver? Suggestions include a pen and paper, some yarn, or a drawing of a web.

THE SQUIRREL

As the final fruitful phase of the cycle before winter returns, there's a swell of energy in September that bridges the human–nature divide, pulling all beings and tasks towards completion. In the wild world, no creature symbolises this better than the squirrel, who bounds along branches gathering nuts and seeds, before hurriedly burying them for winter. Associated with quickness, practicality, and preparation, the squirrel is the epitome of autumn busyness.

In Norse mythology, the squirrel Ratatosk was said to scurry up and down Yggdrasil, the World Tree (explored in 'The Ash Tree' in the April chapter), passing messages between the Underworld and the heavens. The squirrel was also known as the earth messenger of Queen Medb, a medieval Irish warrior queen whose name – linked to an old word for mead – connects her with intoxication, much like the Bramble moon. This idea of being 'under the influence', along with the squirrel's role as a bustling go-between, reflects the potent effects of September's call to action.

For humans, while this flurry of focus can be refreshing and reassuring, it can also lead to a fixation on productivity and achievement. Like other 'fresh start' moments in the cycle, September can bring pressure and expectation – as well as competitiveness driven by the fear of not doing, having, or being enough. In a way, squirrels experience this scarcity-fuelled rivalry too, sometimes pretending to bury their foraged treasures to fool any fellow scavengers who may be watching.

The word 'squirrel' comes from the Greek *skiouros*, meaning 'shadow-tailed'; a name fitting for an animal associated with the incoming darkness of autumn and known in Scottish and Irish folklore as a bringer of rain and snow. Underlying the squirrel's frantic nature lies the wisdom of foresight, reminding us to make ready for what is to come.

Making Space for Slowness

To counter the busy 'squirrel energy' of September, check in with your current to-do list (whether on paper or in your mind) and see if there's anything you can remove or reschedule to create more space. Be really honest with yourself: is everything on your agenda truly necessary – does it all need to be done right now? Outside of work, many expectations and restrictive deadlines can be self-imposed, meaning there's usually a little more room for rest than we might initially think.

THE ACORN

As the seed of the oak tree, the acorn reminds us of the wild world's capacity for transformation, as it grows from its tiny beginnings into the strong, mighty form of the oak. This process of change takes time, but the acorn reminds us of the potential for future growth at a time of year when abundance in nature is beginning to wane. As we likewise navigate change in our own lives, and hold the potential of new beginnings, the acorn offers reassurance that we already have everything we need to thrive contained within us.

Throughout the autumn you might notice squirrels scurrying and seeking out acorns, and so this seed is also connected to gathering and foraging. Just like the squirrel, anything we gather in our lives right now can help us to navigate and sustain ourselves through the winter months ahead, in anticipation of the new cycle and the return of the sun. It's no surprise that in many cultures the acorn is considered a talisman, carried by some in their pocket for luck, or worn as a pendant around the neck to ward off ageing!

Holding Potential

Pick up the first acorn you find and add it to your sacred space, or keep it in your coat pocket throughout autumn and winter. Look at it often, especially when you are thinking of your intentions for next spring and beyond. When spring arrives, plant the acorn and, as you do so, imagine planting all of your intentions and visions for the coming months.

OCTOBER

RELEASE

October swirls in and invites us one final time – before the Wheel turns again – to let go of everything holding us back, to **release** and shed the masks we wear in the world. As animals and trees get ready for the winter months ahead, we begin to refine our reflections and seek clarity, so that we too can move into the next season with ease and a gentle sense of things taking shape beneath the surface. Closing the month is the festival of Samhain, marking both the end and beginning of the Wheel of the Year and encouraging us to delve into our inner layers and reach for our edges in order to stand and live as our true selves.

THE BEECH TREE

Step into a woodland in autumn and you will likely be greeted by the Queen of the Woods – the beech tree – in all her copper-coloured glory. Consort of summer's Oak King, her height and breadth command the landscape, her powerful presence suggestive of strength, courage, and the ability to create our own magic. Her bidding is simple: shed the 'shoulds', discard comparison with others, and embrace your own unique brilliance. This preparation will serve you well once Samhain arrives, offering its annual portal for transformation, and before we reach this pivotal festival of the Wheel, you might like to consider who you wish to be or become in the new cycle that will begin in November.

THE BEECH IS SUGGESTIVE OF STRENGTH, COURAGE, AND THE ABILITY TO CREATE OUR OWN MAGIC.

Providing sustenance for this process, the beech (*Fagus*) is also strongly associated with nourishment. Its genus name derives from the Latin word *phago*, meaning 'to consume or feed', and humans and animals alike have turned to beechnuts over the centuries as a source of food. Nourishing not only the body, but the mind too, the beech is also connected with knowledge. For example, the Welsh witch Cerridwen (in the form of a white sow) was said to have eaten nuts from a sacred beech in order to gain wisdom. As autumn fades and the beech leaves glimmer in the treetops with a final flourish of energy, it is time to dig deep into your own reserves and unearth what you need to sustain yourself in the months ahead.

Your 'Book of Self'

The beech is synonymous with written wisdom in particular, its wood thought to have been used to create the first books; in fact, the term 'book' is derived from *boc*, the Anglo-Saxon word for 'beech'. This month, try creating your own 'book of self': a reflection of who you are in the form of a collection of journal entries or images, or any other form you may wish to explore.

A Sacred Place

With their high, arching branches, beech trees form beautiful, grove-like spaces with a spiritual ambience, and are said to have inspired the building of the first cathedrals. What spaces feel sacred and meaningful to you? Try and cultivate a 'sit spot' in your home or garden that you can return to often, simply to pause, be present, and observe the changes around and within you.

THE HUNTER'S MOON

What is it you seek? This is the question posed by October's lunar cycle. So called because late autumn was traditionally the time for fattening game and hunting deer to provide food for the scarce months ahead, the Hunter's moon is a reminder that winter is on its way, encouraging us to stay alert and equip ourselves with what we need. Coincidentally, it's also a good time of year to look to the skies in search of the constellation Orion, the Hunter, which represents strength and courage – attributes we may desire to help us navigate this time of year.

While this lunar cycle is a time for pursuit, attentiveness, and seeking, the hunter must also be focused, patient, quiet, and able to tap into their intuition, and we are likewise called on to do the same. This is a month to soften and be still, to become calm and quiet, so that we can really hear the answers to the questions we hold in our mind.

Preparing for Winter

Following September's invitation to nourish your body, October is the time to expand this to consider what different parts of you are seeking right now, in preparation for winter. Create a well-being toolkit (whether physical or a list), placing in it anything that might support your mind, body, soul, and spirit to feel energised rather than drained.

Seeking Wisdom from the Hunter's Moon

What are you seeking or hunting?

If you get these things, what will change? How will it make your life different?

What questions are you holding right now?

How can you create more space to listen to your inner wisdom this month?

In what ways do you currently connect with your intuition? How might you deepen this practice?

How might you cultivate a practice of stillness?

THE ENCHANTRESS

As the month of Samhain, or All Hallow's Eve, October brings forth the final and most influential facet of the Mystic archetype: the Enchantress, our inner witch. As the culminating identity not only of autumn, but of the entire yearly cycle, this part of self represents the full spectrum of wisdom held by all the personas within us. Summoning the insights of them all, the Enchantress guides us to reflect on our journey through the seasons and draw our experiences together to feel the full power of what we have learned and who we have become. Channelling this energy of integration and transformation allows us to embrace our personal magic, the unique essence at the heart of our being.

At Samhain, the silken veil between our everyday world and the great beyond of the Otherworld, grows thin, creating a liminal portal suspended in time, within which we are invited to look back in order to move forward. Where September's Weaver offered us the threads of the past, present, and future to help us untangle and reconstruct our stories, the Enchantress turns these stories into spells; powerful incantations that guide us on the path to healing and wholeness. Supported by the whispers of ancestors, whose presence is closely felt as Samhain approaches, our inner sorceress helps us cross the threshold between old and new by honouring the importance of reflection and release.

The Enchantress knows that all beginnings emerge from endings, and that the approaching 'death' of winter is also a crucible of life. As the velvet cloak of darkness envelops our days, calling us to retreat within, we are reminded to trust in the process; to believe in magic.

Find Your Magic

Listen for the voice of your inner Enchantress, and use this guidance to write a 'spell' to invoke your unique magic. Whether in the form of an affirmation, a poem, a song, or something else, use words to craft an incantation you can call upon whenever you need a reminder of who you are and all that you offer to the world.

YOUR SACRED SPACE

What could you add to your sacred space to represent the spellbinding magic of the Enchantress? Suggestions include your spell (see 'Find Your Magic'), a picture of a river, or a symbol of a snake.

THE SERPENT

Known for its long, smooth, undulating roots, the beech tree – explored earlier in this chapter – is said by some to have a serpent dwelling beneath it. A symbol of wisdom and inner knowing in Celtic mythology, the snake is deeply connected with October's theme of letting go, its ability to shed its skin encouraging the release of that which no longer serves us. Frequently linked to witches, either as familiars or shapeshifting disguises, snakes are also traditional signifiers of magic.

One of the most prominent symbolic appearances of the snake throughout history is as the Ouroboros, the Greco-Egyptian portrayal of a serpent eating its own tail, creating an infinite circle that mirrors life's perpetual cycle of destruction and rebirth. In October, this reflects the circular journey through the Wheel of the Year, and the moment of parallel death and renewal represented by Samhain.

Thinking back to the beech tree, the Ouroboros' act of self-consumption also highlights once again the theme of nourishment that is present at this time of year, offering a cautionary reminder that everything we feed ourselves – from food and our surroundings to ideas, words, and relationships – has the power to shape our ever-evolving sense of self.

Shed What No Longer Serves

Write down all the things you 'consume' in your life, paying attention to whether you would consider them to be healing or harmful. As a starting point, you might like to think about: your habits, your diet, sources of entertainment or inspiration (such as books, podcasts, or TV shows), the people you spend time with, social media content, your work and home environments, and any natural or wild spaces you frequent.

Once you've got some ideas noted down, decide which of these things you would like to shed like an old snake skin, and which you would like to keep as an ongoing source of nourishment.

FUNGI

Found in every ecosystem, the world as we know it would not exist without fungi. Their impact is widespread, offering food and medicine for animals and humans, helping to decompose dead matter (such as leaves and insects) and return nutrients to the soil, as well as playing an essential role in plant health. Fungal pathways wind beneath the surface of the soil; mycelia – tiny threads that together form a mycorrhizal network – branch out to reach plants and trees, and this underground support system enables plants to share nutrients and resources and even communicate with each other.

Fungi teach us that everything in nature is interconnected, and that we impact and are impacted by everything around us – human and more-than-human. You might think of this as a ripple in a pond, a spider's web, or a fungal network, but in embracing this ecocentric worldview, our understanding of life shifts dramatically, for in unearthing the wild self, we are also helping to rewild the world around us.

Your Place in the Web

Throw yourself into the childlike nature of this activity! Draw or create a 'mycelial map' on a large piece of paper or card – go freeform and include as many roots or tendrils as you like.

Head out for a walk and tune in to the wild objects that feel meaningful or significant to you, and collect fragments – a leaf, a feather, a flower, a few grains of sand – perhaps aiming for objects that collectively represent all four elements (Earth, Air, Fire, Water).

Now glue or tape all these objects to various points on your map (there are no rules) and also choose one to represent yourself, as a reminder that you are part of the wild world.

ONWARD JOURNEY

As the Wheel of the Year turns and the cycle continues, know that the close of this book is not the end of your journey – in fact, it's just the beginning. Whether you're currently navigating the fallow period of winter, the rising hope of spring, the fullness of summer, or the healing release of autumn, we hope these pages have offered a map to guide you through the seasons of the year, and of your life.

If you ever find yourself feeling lost, remember that unearthing a true understanding of your wild self takes time, and that everyone's pathway will look different. Awareness, curiosity, intuition, and trust will be your most valuable guides as you take the next steps towards deepening your relationship with the wildness within and around you.

Above all, we hope the explorations offered throughout these pages have helped you feel more empowered to move through the coming months and years in your own way, and that this rewilding experience has strengthened your sense of place and purpose in the world.

Let's walk together with love and wild solidarity.

GLOSSARY

Aether The 'celestial' fifth element, which sits alongside the 'terrestrial' elements of Earth, Air, Fire, and Water. It represents different things across various traditions, but in this book it refers to the idea of an intangible and unknowable essence or spirit that connects all life.

archetypal depth psychology Rooted in the work of psychotherapist Carl Jung, this branch of psychology explores the 'depths' of the self and the subconscious through the consideration of inner archetypes.

archetype Carl Jung defined archetypes as universally recognisable patterns, images, symbols, or stories that arise from the 'collective unconscious' – a web of subliminal experience shared by all beings. In their simplest form they represent inner personas or parts of self, such as 'the good girl'.

Celtic tree calendar A symbolic framework that pairs different trees with specific phases of the year, often thought to be a genuine 'ancient' system but likely a more modern idea. The most widely used version is based on *The White Goddess*, a book by 20th-century English writer Robert Graves.

correspondence An association: something that has a symbolic relationship or connection with something else. In our Rewilding Wheel framework, for example, the Earth element is a winter correspondence, while the Water element corresponds with autumn.

deep ecology A social and environmental philosophy founded on a belief in the interconnectedness of all living things and the importance of healing the human–nature divide.

ecocentric A worldview that positions humans as an equal part of the web of life, emphasising that we are not separate from the wild – we are wild. Usually discussed as a nature-aligned alternative to the egocentric perspective, which views humans as outside of, and dominant over, nature.

ecosystem A community of living organisms (such as animals, trees, plants, and humans) all existing in relationship with one another and their physical surroundings as a harmonious whole.

element Earth, Air, Fire, Water, and sometimes Aether: the foundational components of life according to classical and medieval philosophy, and Western spiritual traditions such as Druidry and Wicca. Some or all of the elements also feature in Eastern systems such as Traditional Chinese Medicine or Ayurveda, but have different qualities and associations in these particular contexts.

floriography The art of using the 'language' of flowers to send hidden messages, popularised in Victorian Britain and based on 'floral dictionaries' that assigned symbolic meanings to different flowers.

grounding (earthing) The practice of standing barefoot on soil or grass to connect with the earth's energy, said to balance the body's electrical charge through a two-way flow of electrons.

liminal A state of being 'in between' which is associated with transitions and magic, and often said to bridge the gap between the human world and the Otherworld.

lunar energy Energy imbued with the qualities of the moon, often conflated with the 'feminine': intuitive, gentle, reflective, cyclical, emotional.

Ogham The ancient symbolic language used in Britain and Ireland from around the 4th to 9th centuries, and still seen on the remains of stone monuments today.

oracle deck A collection of cards with symbolic meanings, often used to support reflective practices. Similar to Tarot, but less prescriptive.

ornithomancy 'Bird divination': a practice used by many ancient cultures (particularly Greek and Roman) that interprets the presence and behaviour of specific birds as an omen.

sacred space A place in your home where you can connect with the seasons and with yourself. Whether portable or in a fixed location, use it to display meaningful items that help you honour the wildness within and around you.

solar energy Energy imbued with the qualities of the sun, often conflated with the 'masculine': logical, powerful, action-oriented, practical, purposeful.

soulscape A landscape or habitat used as a symbolic representation of a particular energy, quality, or part of self. For example: the forest soulscape reflects the essence of winter and the inner Sage.

Tarot A collection of cards typically used for divination and/or exploration of your inner world. A tarot deck usually comprises 22 'Major Arcana' (character) cards and 56 'Minor Arcana' (experience) cards.

Wicca A modern, pagan, earth-centred religion that originated in the early 20th century and honours the elements, the Wheel of the Year, rituals and magic.

ABOUT THE AUTHORS

Co-founded by Maddy Winterbrook and Eleanor Cheetham, The Wild Academy creates space amid life's many pressures and expectations to reconnect with the natural world and discover who you truly are. Through practical teaching and soulful self-exploration, our courses, communities, and ceremonies draw on seasonal and cyclical wisdom to help you unearth the wild within.

Maddy specialises in supporting the growth of wild-hearted women. She holds a Postgraduate Diploma in Coaching and Mentoring, through which she developed her nature-led approach, and is currently training as an integrative therapist. Endlessly fascinated by the complexities of human experience, she is most at home exploring the depths and shadows of the self.

Eleanor is a multi-hyphenate creative and weaves threads of storytelling, archetypes, mythology, and earth-based spirituality in her work as a writer, teacher, publisher, and designer. A trained teacher, she has a Masters in Creative Writing and is inspired by place-based folklore and language, as well as the soulful relationships that our ancestors had with the land.

To discover more about Maddy and Eleanor's work, please see:

www.thewildacademy.co.uk

thewildacademy.substack.com

www.instagram.com/thewildacademy

RESOURCES

Clarissa Pinkola Estés, *Women Who Run With the Wolves: Myths and Stories of the Wild Woman Archetype*, Rider, 2022

David Abram, *Becoming Animal: An Earthly Cosmology*, Vintage Books, 2010

Glennie Kindred, *Earth Wisdom: A Heartwarming Mixture of the Spiritual, the Practical, and the Proactive*, Hay House, 2011

Joanna Macy, *World as Lover, World as Self*, Parallax Press, 2021

Martin Shaw, *Courting the Wild Twin*, Chelsea Green Publishing, 2020

Robin Wall Kimmerer, *Braiding Sweetgrass: Indigenous Wisdom, Scientific Knowledge, and the Teachings of Plants*, Milkweed Editions, 2020

Rosie Steer, *Slow Seasons: A Creative Guide to Reconnecting with Nature the Celtic Way*, Bloomsbury, 2023

Satish Kumar, *Soil, Soul, Society: A New Trinity for Our Time*, Ivy Press, 2013

Sharon Blackie, *If Women Rose Rooted: A Life-Changing Journey to Authenticity and Belonging*, September Publishing, 2016

A VERBENA BOOK
© David and Charles, Ltd 2025

Verbena is an imprint of David and Charles, Ltd, Suite A, Tourism House, Pynes Hill, Exeter, EX2 5WS

Text © Maddy Winterbrook and Eleanor Cheetham 2025
Layout © David and Charles, Ltd 2025

First published in the UK and USA in 2025

A catalogue record for this book is available from the British Library.

ISBN-13: 9781446315712 paperback
ISBN-13: 9781446315729 EPUB

This book has been printed on paper from approved suppliers and made from pulp from sustainable sources.

Printed in China through Asia Pacific Offset for: David and Charles, Ltd, Suite A, Tourism House, Pynes Hill, Exeter, EX2 5WS

10 9 8 7 6 5 4 3 2 1

Publishing Director: Ame Verso
Senior Commissioning Editor: Lizzie Kaye
Managing Editor: Jeni Chown
Editor: Jessica Cropper
Project Editor: Caroline West
Lead Designer: Sam Staddon
Designers: Giulia Sandri & Jess Pearson
Pre-press Designer: Susan Reansbury
Illustrations: Rachael Roux
Production Manager: Beverley Richardson

Layout of the digital edition of this book may vary depending on reader hardware and display settings.